FallingOff
theCatwalk

RobertN. Reincke

Spunky Books

Falling Off the Catwalk
By Robert N. Reincke

Published by Spunky Books
West Hollywood, CA
spunkybooks.com

All of the stories are true and all the characters are real, but the
names were changed to protect the privacy of the individuals.

LIBRARY OF CONGRESS CATALOGING-IN-PUBLICATION
DATA

Reincke, Robert
Falling Off the Catwalk/ Robert N. Reincke

ISBN 978-0-9794241-1-3
Library of Congress Control Number: 2008905137

Covers: Robert Reincke, Milan 1993 and San Diego 1994

Design and Layout By: Michael J. Mackel
Editor: Toni Kelley

FIRST EDITION
2008

To Mike

&

In Memory of my Father

Author'sNote

Painstaking effort has gone into writing this memoir authentically. Information from extensive journals, a daily planner, photographs, a tape recording, and video recordings (some of which are online at the publisher's website) recreated the events and emotions described herein. Written journal entries include original errors to enhance the reader's sense of the author's state of mind. Similarly, transcripts of videos and tapes were not edited to correct speech. The author relied on memory sparingly and, where relied upon, made every effort to be thoroughly honest. Name changes to protect identity are the only fictitious information.

Contents

Ring the bells you still can ring
Forget your perfect offering
There's a crack in everything
That's how the light shines in

—LEONARD COHEN

Prologue

Tape-recorded January 1991: *Last night we slept together in the waterbed. Last night it was a little different. We did lay very closely—constantly something was touching. Petey upside down and me. I didn't really get much rest. I could see his silhouette on the other side of the bed at night with the look of, with the look of, ahhhh...repressed anxiety—as was mine. Intensely repressed anxiety. But we repressed it. Or neither one of us pounced on the other with some sexual acts. The difference is that we love each other. I love him and I've told him that. HE loves me and he's told me that too. That was the main feeling LOVE. That was more powerful than sex, the drive for sex. The part of our bodies that touched. You could sense every single bone, every single muscle. It felt free, alive, very comfortable, very comfortable, very cozy. It was a positive thing. A good thing.*

I talked to him today. I saw him, and we worked out together today. The whole time I was fighting a hard-on. So was he, you could tell—the kind of way he reaches his balls and adjusts them. I had a hard-on when I talked to him on the phone. I masturbated three times—once this morning in the shower and twice this evening. There's no sense in denying it. There's absolutely no sense in denying it. I mean I've already written it. I'm a bisexual. I definitely have homosexual tendencies. I'm in love with Petey. Petey is in love with me. Even though we slept together we didn't do anything. We're both just reposed, cautious, wary...and this is new. Definitely a very new feeling or at least we're acknowledging the feeling...I can have a relationship with Petey and the friendship will last forever and the girls will come later. There's always a girl.

...Here we are in the midst of a relationship beyond friendship. But I can deal with it, and I think Petey can too. We're both cool. Just be ourselves man. Just totally be ourselves. I can't let any of his family know. And we didn't really have sex. Not that we didn't want to. We did want to. I heard him mumble. Are we going to do it? I don't feel like it tonight. Then we separated. Then started touching. That's the fear. The fear. I'm really happy because I really love him and I've never

had a real relationship, a sexual relationship with anybody I've loved. I've had sex with girls but never really loved them. The Dracula movie is on. Dracula is getting blown up from the sun. I'm going to shut the tape off.

FallingOff
theCatwalk

FlyingToParis 01

In 1993, I was 29, looked 22, claimed to be a straight, born-again Christian, and recently had stopped going to Alcoholics Anonymous meetings. Blessed with great looks (which I had asked God for in a childhood prayer) I had wavy, shoulder-length hair bleached from the sun and saltwater of six years of surfing. My body was in great shape due to this, yoga, and endless escapist workouts in the campus gym of my employer—the San Diego Plotter Division of the Hewlett-Packard Company. I had, by all outside appearances, what seemed a great life that I created for myself by my mid-twenties—a condominium near the ocean (in Encinitas—north San Diego County) a soft-top, mag-tired Jeep Wrangler, pretty ex-girlfriends, and a stable, practical, decent-paying, Fortune 500 corporate job. As I approached 30, however, the illusion I had created for myself began increasingly to show signs of its own incredibility.

I had chosen my profession—purchasing—based upon a sales pitch by my undergraduate university that promised me the potential of not-too-demanding coursework, high-salary, and the upward mobility that I believed was the entitlement of all Americans. It did not suit me (a personality test I later took ranked purchasing well beneath art and spiritual pursuits at the bottom of characteristic interests). Although paid relatively well for my age, I found myself in a condo I couldn't afford; in a car that was also too expensive for me; and working in a cubicle where I felt suffocated. I was clearly lacking the drive and blind ambition, which my even younger coworkers possessed, but felt embittered by not being promoted. Clearly, I had other and more demanding issues too—my pot smoking and drinking binges were at odds with my life; and, importantly, I was clearly back in denial about being gay.

1

As the years at my corporate job progressed, I floundered in and out of sobriety. It became clear that, despite having pursued even more education with a Masters Degree in Business Administration, my cost of living was rapidly outpacing my earnings. I was experiencing a net negative return on my output as I increasingly disliked what I was doing. On another level, I wasn't any longer secure in the belief that I would be content if I were to achieve my original material and heterosexual familial aspirations. Eventually, after convincing myself I had met a prerequisite of one-year sober time (I rationalized that my one slip on pot didn't count), I took solace in speaking with a trained therapist.

Clarity about my job was one revelation that resulted from our sober sessions. Perhaps the reason I found myself working for a computer engineering company was more to suit my family's expectations (my mother had been a computer science teacher and my father an engineer) than my own. Soon I began the desperate search for a new career. Doors remained shut, and opportunities to move up, over, or out, either were out of reach or paid less than I was receiving. As my increased un-medicated (by pot, alcohol, or AA meetings) rage grew, so too did inner emotional screams to escape what I thought was my Yuppie exile. For a time I thought of joining the Peace Corps to help rebuild Russia, until a coworker reported that my alcoholic recovery seemed to be coming along all right. The ensuing investigation of my sobriety spooked me away from their program.

One of my last girlfriends—an amateur photographer—advised that one option for new employment was to become a model. I thought this wasn't such a bad idea since, as a teenager, I had for years taken great interest in magazine and newspaper clippings of fashionable women and well dressed, or shirtless, well-defined men. I had always felt paranoid that people stared at me, which I hypothesized was because they either knew I was high (when I was or wasn't), perceived me to be oddly different, or simply because they found me extraordinarily handsome. That being the case, I thought why not see if I couldn't get paid for this God-gifted natural exhibitionism of good looks. Taking her advice, I agreed to a "test" photo shoot using her as my photographer. I later took the photos to a San Diego modeling agency she had also recommended, and I was, to my great delight, accepted.

The agency suggested that if I really wanted to give modeling a shot, Europe would be the place for me to get some pictures and work. I was getting older—I thought I was experiencing an early mid-life crisis, just as my father had for many years—and the agency confirmed my fears that this might be my last shot. Besides, the fashion work that my exotic, European good looks qualified me for was sparse in San Diego. They told me the more mundane, commercial photography work that existed there required a bland, faux-collegiate, athletic look.

I immediately cut my hair, began working out with fervor, and took additional test shoots with photographers suggested by the agency. I would often arrange my work cubicle with desk lamp on and spreadsheets carefully placed in a haphazard manner to leave the impression that I was called away suddenly to a meeting when, in fact, I was working out or visiting with an agent or photographer. One afternoon, in an effort to expand my modeling options, I drove up to Orange County to meet another agent. He also signed me, and further confided—despite risking that I might never return to him like other "boys"—that Europe was a prudent choice if I could muster it, for only there could I obtain the kind of tear sheets from printed magazines and test photo shoots that I would need to develop a modeling "book" and build a career.

He sent me to three L.A.-based test photographers who took increasingly better photo shoots, as I learned more about how to interact with the camera and express the feel that the photographer was trying to elicit. The experiences provoked other feelings as well. Instructed by my early test photographer to wear either outlandish designer fashions or a sexy, urban, bad-boy look that didn't suit me, I felt oddly embarrassed, exposed, and victimized. This provided one of many erroneous excuses for increased drinking, which began to occur more frequently around activities associated with my new profession.

The third test-photographer's shoot had a very fortunate conclusion. The clothes that he recommended for me—Armani suits (which I bought with my credit card, hid the tags while we shot, and later promptly returned)—fit what I considered my elegant, classical, personal style, and made me feel comfortable. His choosing the shoot location on the beach provided the peace that I experienced near the sea. The photographer, who would later become my roommate, knew how to pose me so that I looked vulnerable, expressive, and sexy. The result was a series of photos that would allow me entrance to the world of international, male fashion modeling and transform my life forever.

I soon thought the time was right to take a risk, go to Paris (where I had a friend who said I could stay with her free), find an agency, and get work as a model. I wasn't astute enough to realize that the international fashion industry was suffering from both an economic recession and a dramatic change in consumer tastes brought on by the demise of the yuppie era of conspicuous consumption (the 80's). I would soon experience the ramifications of both. But I didn't care. My needs to free myself from my own materialistic trap seemed too urgent to wait.

Additionally, my closest friends from graduate school and my early years at Hewlett-Packard had left the county, leaving me without familiar friends. The one acquaintance I hung out with when I went to AA meetings was busy getting sober after I had fully relapsed. Two new friends included a girl, Shannell, who had offered me my first jug of Gallo wine when I told myself the first of many times that I was not an alcoholic and could control my drinking, and a man, Ian, I slept with after drinking too much shortly thereafter—I found him irritating because he *seemed* gay and was too fond of me. Additionally, my work had recently caused me to transfer to another cubicle in the Research and Development Department where I sat alone for hours doing nothing while waiting for the lab project I was to work on to start ramping up (projected at another six months hence). Luckily, the move offered me the opportunity to remove my personal effects without anybody noticing.

Telling no one my real intent, I requested a two-week "vacation" from work. This allowed the option to return if my efforts at being a model didn't materialize. I then promptly moved all of my personal effects—scrap books, journals and photo albums—from my condominium into a storage unit. I left it otherwise fully furnished with plants, stereo system, waterbed, surfboards, and books that included a compilation of all the religions of the world and "The Big Book" of *Alcoholics Anonymous*—both unread. Finally, I set up a system whereby the bank automatically deducted my mortgage and car payments from my checking account. This had less than $1,000 in it—my entire life savings.

The next morning I grabbed my well-packed suitcases and the video recorder that I used as a video journal and walked out the door of my condo. I then dropped off a spare set of keys to the real-estate agency I had instructed to rent it should I call. I later wrote down in my daily organizer (a "Franklin Planner" in which I documented my present activities more often than planned future events) that I stopped by Miracles Cafe, which was appropriately named for what I hoped would follow, and had a final mocha before leaving Encinitas forever. I then had Shannell drive me to the airport in my Jeep, which she kept, promising to send monthly payments to the bank should I not return (she had recently just recovered from a drunk driving charge and had no car). As I sat on the airplane, I opened a book of blank pages I had thriftily retrieved from the trash bin of the Marcom Department of my HP division where I had one of my last unsuccessful interviews. Feeling (as I wrote several hours later) I was "carried forward in the palm of God or by some unknown Karmic force," I penned my first enthusiastic entry on the first page of what would become many books, of my new life:

5

It's the 27th of May, exactly five months to the day of my thirtieth day of birth (How ironic, except I take irony seriously). I'm on my way to Paris. We're 30,000 plus feet above the desert floor right now and will be flying over Tucson and El Paso before we disembark in Houston from San Diego. Somehow this seems oddly appropriate, flying over parts of the still desolate and unconquered wild west, including Tijuana Mexico, on my way to the epitome of civilized life - the heart of the international fashion industry, for what, I'm almost too frightened to admit to myself, could hopefully become a new life for me.

This is the most prepared I have been for a trip of any kind. I've spent the last two weeks planning and packing. All of my personal things are in storage and the storage unit is paid through August. I have nothing to have to come back to. My place is available for rent immediately at a phone call and the real estate person has the keys. My major bills are covered and minor ones being taken care of. Even my newspaper and auto insurance are on indefinite hold. My homeowner's association fees are the only unpaid bills. All else is covered until July.

Most importantly is that everything personal of mine at work has been cleaned out and stored; all files emptied and any personal computer information copied and deleted from my hard drive. I am free to terminate with a phone call and manage my home and car from abroad. This is almost petrifying for me because I know it is the time of my life in which I need to do this.

Hewlett-Packard, though I officially still work for it, is already part of my past; part of my University of San Diego Masters degree in business administration; part of my Michigan State University Bachelors degree in that odd, completely unrelated to anything whatsoever near my identity, major – Materials and Logistics Management with an emphasis on Purchasing; all part and parcel of the earlier me vision that is now safely packed away in storage only to be reviewed as nostalgia. For, I am no longer that young naive Michigan boy on the inside or outside.

The earth below is completely desolate and barren. Praise God his will be done. Solace - Termination, what a blissful thought. What another absolute marvel and irony. I'm reading Generation X: Tales for an Accelerated Culture above the clouds with my felt blow-up head cushion skewed around my neck. I'm reading fabulously funny accounts of my life and that of my friends.

The disgusting thought of [other HP employees and engineers] crossed my mind - so trapped...I think of [a coworker] that old man - almost 40 years - with the mongo-lithic corporation - sitting - pining away in his zombie clone death freeze at his desk, spying on my telephone conversations. I also heard him bragging that he hadn't taken a vacation in two years. I thought - poor, poor man...get a life... please. Forty years and he doesn't leave that dark, sick building for even a vacation - how abhorrent.

Back to reading Generation X. I couldn't have written it better. As Debbie, the little coffee-girl [and another former ex-girlfriend] said, "It's scary because it's so close to my own life." The clouds below me are identical to those on the cover of the book - yet another irony? I meant no harm to HP. I'm not leaving anything undone that hasn't been undone already.

ICameToJesus 02

Iarrived in Paris early Friday morning, and, according to my journal, first took a bus where a "very helpful French woman" helped me stamp my ticket, then "a cab where a very friendly cab driver helped me after stealing a 30% tip." I then walked a short distance on a narrow cobblestone street through two extremely large, wooden doors into the courtyard of the old building where my friend, Eve, lived. Once there I climbed up several flights of an ancient circular stairwell, arched and grooved with troughs where so many feet had walked for centuries. I grabbed a hidden key and let myself into the empty apartment.

Eve, who was not there at the time, had been completing her Masters of Comparative Law degree as I completed my Masters of Business Administration at the University of San Diego, and then returned to work in her native France. She prided herself on her joie d' vivre and casual demeanor that she felt made her more sympathetic to American culture than her own. The apartment was tiny, consisting of a small sink, toaster, and mini-refrigerator next to a bathroom that contained all its elements in a space the size of a small closet. The main area contained bookshelves, a futon, that took up most of the room, with blankets at its foot for me. Admittedly stark in her furnishings, Eve's one extravagance was a big, pink satin, down coverlet on her futon. When I finally saw her, she made it quite clear that she wouldn't mind sharing her fluffy bed if I would be so inclined.

Without that to worry about for the moment, I commenced with other more pertinent responsibilities. A girl I had met on the plane told me that the following Monday was a "Christian holiday," and that all the agencies would be closed, leaving me less time to fulfill my mission. I no sooner dropped my bags then I began to call the agencies recommended to me to set up appointments. According to the journal, I wrote later, the following scene unfolded:

Journal May 29, 1993 Sometime after Midnight: *Called the modeling agency Bananas, Wilhelmina, and then Glamour where a woman named Catherine said stop by after 3:00 p.m. at the earliest. Thank God I did at exactly 3:00, because shortly thereafter all these male models started showing up. I would have been thoroughly intimidated if I had shown up late. After the calls, I had lunch at a cafe just down the street from Eve's four hundred plus year old apartment building (Pasta, red wine, espresso, and garlic mozzarella bread - it was wonderful). Two gay men came in and one sat at my table and made statements about me being a gorgeous model—a good sign. (People all speak French to me here immediately - even in the airport they waived me through as a Frenchman - another good sign). I [then] visited Wilhelmina where the agent said, "Darling, don't you know...it goes like this...First Milan, THEN Paris, then New York..." The next stop was the Metro—FDR exit to Montaigne to Francois 1er: The beautiful people – beautiful and expensive, it seems to me – district nearby where Eve works. Once at Glamour, Catherine asked me quite bluntly what my plans were...stay in town or to go. I said I was thinking of going to Milan. She said, "Yes, you HAVE to go to Milan." It was slow in Paris. Have I seen other agencies?" I said she was the first and smoked a cigarette I had borrowed from another agent sitting at the large round table. She then said she loved the test pictures I had taken in L.A. and brought with me, and would call me tonight. I didn't hear from her and will call her Tuesday morning. She said she had to think about it. By the time I left, the room was full with four or five male models. I left without saying goodbye to any of them. They all intently stared at me. I was too tired to be intimidated. They seemed to put importance into me. I was glad to walk off and made a perfect left onto rue Francais and then Montaigne to the corner of these beautiful golden gates and the Metro exit. I walked to a bench and noticed the Arche de Triumphe to my right as I sat below a beautiful fully green tree. I couldn't have chosen a more perfect stop to gather my now completely jet lagging exhausted and actually dizzy thoughts. It was 4:00 PM. Banana's was next. I felt I had all I could for the day and realized that if Wilhelmina couldn't get me work - Banana's - who I scheduled right off the plane - certainly couldn't either. I took the Metro anyway. By the time I got to*

9

the stop I should have taken, it was so far from the cool spots in town, and I was so hot and lagged out of my senses that I immediately turned around and headed back. Oh, on my way, I had stopped at a stop where I saw the Eiffel Tower by chance - so much for sightseeing. Just perfect - all I could have ever imagined. Seeing and discovering Paris as I did L.A. by working it. Somehow that brings so much more satisfaction to me.

Anyhow on the way back as I stood crowded in with the others—quiet and tired actually exhausted—a man came in, crippled and pushy, spouting something and then asking for donations. Looks of disgust, embarrassment and pity prevailed, including from me. Then a musician came aboard. I guess I got the right compartment somehow. We all basically ignored him too. No one even bothered to clap. One of his words - the only I could make out was - America… No idea if it was good or bad. I continued to pretend I was not one and tried to fit in as best as I could. I think I've been successful at it. The Parisians looked so tired and frazzled. Their life is hard and their drinking is what makes them impatient, unpredictable, and surly. I am comfortable with this thought. And they are comfortable with me. We accept each other here. I love Paris. I exited - got lost and finally made it home. Oh yeah - until the exiting point I kept thinking all of the events of my day were happening just as they should - as if fate had something to say about what had been going on.

I fell asleep at 6 p.m., unaware if or when Eve returned, and did not record it. The following day I was "still in love with the idea of Paris" and spent the entire day sightseeing with a girl I met on the airplan, Simone. Sensing that Eve was jealous, I bought her a gift, but still decided to spend that evening out with my new friend and two of her girlfriends at a big disco. I had never been to a big city disco before and was interested in experiencing one. My only experiences with bars until then were surfer beer joints and college bars that ended with us all singing *Bye, Bye, Miss American Pie* in a big circle. Going out with a group of friendly girls made me feel comfortable, and, my friend had told me, increased my chances of getting in with the modeling crowd.

The disco called L'Arc was, in fact, near the Arc de Triomphe. It was the most popular disco in the city—rivaled only by the racier

Queen. As predicted, we were allowed into a large, smoky room, crowded with the crème de la crème of French club-goers, young models, and the fashion industry elite. I made my way up to the bar and ordered what I later recorded as "a very expensive Perrier water," which I bought in my continued, unsuccessful efforts to control how much alcohol I would eventually consume. I must not have bought my new friends a drink as I would scarcely have been able to afford it (I have no receipts of that although I have receipts of nearly everything else).

I found myself on the dance floor observed by a pretty, but slightly older woman. At first, I ignored her, not feeling comfortable with her directness. According to the details I recorded in a video of myself, shirtless, retelling the story the next day, she asked if I was a model. I said, "no, but I was trying to be." I made my way to her table, which I noted had a full bottle of vodka on it. She poured me a drink and talked to me in between kisses on the cheek as models and passers-by showed their courtesies and tried to gain her attentions.

Etienne, a former model, told me she was a Parisian "Boo-k-airrrr" (agent), which increased the importance I placed on her. My secret, lifelong dream was to be discovered and ripped away from the mediocrity that existed around me (before tedious work it was gray Michigan). Even as a little boy on a trip to Universal Studios, I half expected a producer to pull me off the tram and discover me. There at the bar, I ate her affections and yearned for more despite feeling uneasy in the setting, and with the sexual nature of her assertiveness. Drinking from the endless bottles of vodka and bursting with the inner acknowledgement that what was happening had always meant to happen, I listened intently as she told me what wonderful opportunities I had as a model. "I must go to [the agency] Frog," she told me, and "the agency Boss was good in New York." She could help, she confirmed, as well as find me a place to live, possibly even with her for the time being.

She took me onto the dance floor and groped me as we danced

11

close to one another, making me feel odd that we were the only two beneath the disco ball and above the glowering multi-colored lights. Having lost the girls I came with—Simone had told me that she thought Etienne's behavior was disgusting—I left for another bar with Etienne and then on a sightseeing tour of Paris in her Mercedes. As night ebbed into morning, she offered to take me to Eve's or, if I chose, to her apartment in the elitist sixteenth district. This was Paris after all, so I decided to go along with the adventure.

Once at her extremely well equipped apartment—replete with current, well-posed photos of her that seemed more a lonely reminder of her past—she played CDs of Billy Holiday and Cat Stevens, which reminded me of a happy period in my life. She then drew a bubble bath, gave me a blowjob, and jerked me off, according to a Franklin entry for that day. I was pleased that we didn't have full intercourse, but got zero sleep, which bothered me—the details recounted in my video as follows:

Video May 30: *Touchy feeling. I don't know who she is. She sucked my dick a bit last night and then gave me a hand-job. We didn't have full intercourse, which is good. But, I would have done anything I guess. I didn't know what the deal was. I didn't know. Can she help me? Would I need to sleep with her to get help? We used each other completely. I was used and she was. I used her to find out what it was I could get from her, and she used me. She wanted my body. She wanted me. She thinks I'm hot and I am hot. I am hot. She says, "I understand why you want to be a model." No one else seems to understand. She says, "you make it in the next three or four years and that's it it's over. You either do it now or it's over." I know I can't go back to work at Hewlett-Packard. Fuck that. No way. If I go back to San Diego she says she'll visit me. I said, "I hate working in a cubicle for $40,000 a year." She says, "you can make $40,000 in two days in modeling." I don't want to dick around. I'm ready to go. I'm already a different person in two days. I got here on Friday and it's only Sunday. This experience has left an indelible mark on my personality—my psyche—that will never go away. I'm here to stay. Who I am take it or leave it. It's me. I feel good about myself.*

The next morning her sister, another young man, and a woman

(all who spoke only French) came over, and together we drove to the countryside to a place called Roumbeillet near where her brother lived. This all made me nervous as I began to think that I was introduced into the family a bit prematurely and didn't otherwise know what to make of it. We smoked cigarettes, drank wine, and nibbled on fruit and goat cheese in a lovely cafe that made me feel as if I were part of Renoir's painting, *The Boating Party*. Despite the majesty of the moment, I felt like an imposter while everyone else was sincerely having a better time than I. Etienne then moved from her chair, sat on my lap, and wiggled around. I felt embarrassed for I was raised to respect good table manners. Soon I would learn that the fashion industry elite enjoyed acting out in every social situation they could (it made them seem superior).

After lunch, she squeezed my ass with the full force of her hand as we walked around the chateau in the park and admired the white swans. I may have intensely disliked my role as a businessperson, but being a sexual plaything didn't feel completely right either. Nonetheless, I tried to remain aloof and worldly, resigned to the opinion that if this was what I needed to learn, I'd go along with it for the time being. Once in the city I chose to take the Metro immediately back to Eve's instead of driving any further with Etienne. Eve wasn't there, as I would discover was usual, so I took off my pants to reveal my green plaid boxer shorts and my shirt and sat on her pink coverlet reiterating every detail of my amazing first Saturday for posterity and eventually fell asleep.

After finally getting twelve hours of good rest, I awoke to "the Christian Holiday" of Monday, May 31. The Second Day of Pentecost (or *Le Pentecote*) celebrated the visitation of the Holy Spirit upon the apostles, the people, and the church. Though a national holiday in France and one meant to therefore embrace all of the country's Christians, it meant nothing to any of the people I knew nor to me.

My earliest memory of a God consciousness was a dreaded fear of what it would be like if I were to die and go nowhere; if all consciousness would end and I were to lose all memory or recognition; of an empty, dark void. Never exposed to the concept of being *everything*, I feared the thought of being nothing. My mother, who once taught Sunday school, introduced me to Methodism at an early age, where during occasional Sunday services and confirmation classes I learnt much about Protestant Christianity. My father's side of the family exposed me to Catholicism. Dad had once wanted to be a priest but dropped out of seminary for some unexplained reason—he first became an atheist, then an agnostic, and finally attended Methodist church on holidays to please my mom. Around the time I hit puberty, I took a fervent approach to Christianity.

One day, feeling alone and isolated, far from the friends I had left behind when my family moved, I switched the TV onto a Billy Graham crusade. I had already read a Bible called *The Way* that my godmother had gifted me, but now wanted to hear what Billy had to say. I was told that if I believed and prayed to Jesus that I would go on living when I died. I imagined a great paradise called "heaven," high above the white clouds and away from the horrifyingly bland, uninspiring, metropolitan Detroit area where I lived. I wanted to be saved and to do what was right. I wanted to go on remembering and live, forever comfortable, in an eternity where I didn't feel harassed, bullied, or taunted. I fell to my knees and prayed. I then called the Billy Graham people and shortly thereafter received some literature. From this, I realized more fully I had been what they described as "born again." I understood, too, that I needed to continually give my life to Jesus, which meant that I had to continually pray that Jesus would have all of me; that my body, mind, soul, and spirit belonged to this spirit/ person who was all-seeing and all-knowing.

I have a melodramatic personality, so I took this belief system a step further. One day, I found myself hanging naked from the circular staircase of our family home, in an effort to do as many pull-ups as I could because the feeling of exercising naked and smelling the newly emerging body odor from my arm pits gave me an incredible feeling.

I laid a newspaper clipping of a bulky marine doing pushups on the floor below me for motivation (looking at muscular guys gave me more drive), and pulled myself up with great gusto. Suddenly I felt an odd sensation as I noticed that my foot became wet with a white, sticky substance that I didn't recognize. At first, I was fearful, but then thought about how pleasant the feeling was. Taking myself into the bedroom, I experimented with what I noticed was an engorged penis, as it had been shortly before the strange emission. Using common sense, I decided to stroke it. The feelings were so remarkable that I felt they were spiritual and had to be from God. Looking towards my bookshelf, I noticed a crucifix that my paternal grandmother had gifted me. I prayed to Jesus that he have my body, the feelings I was having, and everything about my "sex" for his glory.

Time progressed and I became ever more stringent in my faith, believing that I needed to uphold all the laws of God and man. This created further conflict as some of the laws of man were very difficult to follow—like the speed limit—and some of the laws of God didn't work in my culture—like the rule against the wearing of garments made out of blended materials. Interestingly, I clung to Biblical tenets that seemed to speak negatively about gays and money—two issues that preoccupied my subconscious and conscious mind. My increased drinking coincided with the glaring contrast between my beliefs and what I felt was true for me. I was in a constant state of limbo and conflict—I couldn't come out (or, interestingly, be wealthy, based upon my interpretation of a biblical verse concerning a wealthy man's chances of going to heaven compared with a camel going through the eye of the needle). By the time I had arrived in Paris, it was imperative that I not waiver in my beliefs and openly acknowledge my faith, in order to ensure that I achieved salvation—having remembered Jesus, He would remember me, I thought. This was my primary religious approach besides forced abstinence from gay thoughts and actions.

I spent the Second Day of Pentecost having brunch with a successful family man and business owner, Hugo—another friend of mine from graduate school at my Catholic graduate university—and left feeling at odds with the differences I saw between his life and mine. Later, I rode alone up the escalator of the famous Pompidou Center of the Arts and looked out over the city below while I pondered my fate. I was in Paris trying to become a model. Although a part of me was envious of him, I knew I didn't want my friend's life, and knew that I didn't want the life I had back in the States. Modeling could help, I told myself. By modeling, I could "learn of other cultures," while "pursuing my painting and sculpting interests, learn languages," and most importantly, "learn about myself," I optimistically journaled. "Comfort and happiness in my sexuality—not a wild, but an intense sexuality"—was what I most wanted to "discover, release, enjoy, and come to terms with," I profoundly wrote in my journal that evening. For the first time I was honest with myself about my true mission. I would soon repress it and forget.

Reinvigorated, the following day (Tuesday, June 1, 1993) I continued to take actions necessary to become a model and visited two of the top Parisian agencies. The agency Elite liked my pictures, but for them to take me on they would need more. They suggested I start with a smaller agency and then come back in about three months when I had a more substantial book—"Fuck!" I recorded in my journal. Beyond the gilded gates of a former French mansion, into the intimidating MGM agency, the story was the same. I was told that guys apparently came into their agency with bound tear sheets that measured into the inches (the agents loved to enhance this statement with a hand held up, forefinger and thumb significantly spaced apart) and that I was possibly too short (that although I was 5 foot 11¾ inches, 6 foot was the minimum). Both agencies also recommended that I see Frog (the agency), which began to sound like my salvation.

By the end of the day, after smoking three cigarettes—my max for any given day—I returned to Eve's feeling as if I had "lost my karma—ashamed, tired, frustrated, and depressed." Rebelliously, I took off my shirt and pants (to get out of the outfit I had worn in an effort to "fit into Parisian culture"), put on my surfer shorts and a hoop earring (in the pierced left, or "straight," ear), and turned on the video recorder to motivate myself as follows:

Video June 2: *I can't go back to San Diego. I'll die…Oh God help me. He hasn't helped me. Maybe Frog will help me…you know I think there's still hope…I've always got hope. I'm an endless chain of hope. I have that inner strength to keep going when the going seems endless, it's been endless, and it will be endless forever until I die and I'm gone from this earth. I have hope. I'm a survivor and I need to forge my way. It's not easy. If it were easy everybody would do it. If you're weak you just give up - you do, you can't do it. If you're strong you keep going, and you keep going, and you keep going, and you don't stop ever. I don't stop. Never. And this is my ray of sunshine. It's not looking good right now, so I keep going…Tomorrow I get to do this Frog thing. And everyone says Frog. Frog. Frog. Frog. There is potential. Everyone seems to think it's possible. I don't need doom and gloom. I don't need to go to Milan. All this doom and gloom bullshit. Fuck that…no way…It's not over. It's not over till it's over. You know what a good sign is? I still have five hundred French Francs left. Not like six. I have five hundred. It's one hundred dollars. It's like not a lot. Especially when I spent one hundred and ten for lunch.*

In concluding what turned into an extensive recording, I looked directly into my camera and said with feigned comfort that I wasn't a drug addict or alcoholic, because "I am really down and exhausted, yet don't feel like drinking right then or using (pot)." I voiced that this was "a big step," and it was. Not because it was true, but because it gave me another excuse to drink with abandon from then on out.

Just then, Eve, wearing her customary big, gaudy, and meant-to-be-purposefully-over-the-top earrings and a flashy, red business suit walked in and interrupted my recording. After returning from my first very nice Parisian meal paid for by her, I felt guilty about sleeping on the floor at the foot of her bed. "Would you mind if I lay in bed with you?" I asked. "But, of course," was her reply.

The next morning I visited Glamour, Bananas, PH1, Success, and the all-important Frog. None of them took me. Reasons included there was an economic "crisis" in Paris, and with it being show season—the busiest and most challenging time of the year—I would easily get lost in the shuffle. Things would be different, I was told, if I was either taller, had a bigger book, or had come earlier to build my book in preparation for this most competitive time. I determined to accept my situation and not take it personally—"...whatever was *was*," I later wrote. Egged on by Parisian salesclerks, I bought a tight fitting pair of red pants that I thought I might wear into the clubs in the future, and later chastised myself ("I feel like Jim Morrison but at the same time like a faggot," I recorded in my camera) for buying them. I also visited a church—the American Episcopal Church of Paris—where "I heard some wild gothic music and prayed for God's will for me." It was to be just one of many churches and cemeteries where I would seek solace. Thinking that "if I went back to the States I'd have to quit my job anyway," I resolved instead to take the train to Milan that night, and try my chances there. Eve escorted me to the station and waved goodbye. I promised her I would be back—one way or another.

I'mNotGay 03

I arrived in Milan early Thursday, June 3, "feeling warm and sticky" and looking disheveled from my journey. I found a residential hotel near the city center, directly next door to the bell tower of an old church. No sooner did I drop my bag than I called the first agency on the list of top agents and agencies I had. Mary Stella, the head booker at Joy, scheduled an appointment for that afternoon. I then called Ugly People and spoke with a booker named Hobbes, who cleverly told me it was best to see him as soon as possible. I told him I was wearing a baseball cap and needed to freshen up. He told me that he could "see through the dirt of my all-night travels." We set the appointment for 11 a.m., just before the one I was to have had with Mary Stella.

I took a cab to Ugly People's address and felt reassured by the tranquil, suburban surroundings and the lush, green park that stood next to it. I entered through a narrow lobby that overlooked a sophisticated booking area surrounded by walls of inlaid, dark wood. A well-dressed, effeminate, forty-something man sat at the long, rectangular booking table. Across from him sat Antonella, his assistant—an olive-complexioned Italian woman with dramatically long, full hair and a feisty attitude. Hobbes introduced himself with his characteristic bold mannerisms and sultry, deep voice and Antonella said "Ciao." He then showed me around the agency. There in a back boardroom I saw the wall of models' composite cards present in all agencies. The models were all men, and most of them I could recognize from the pages of *GQ*, *Details*, *Esquire*, *Men's Fitness*, and other major men's fashion publications of the time. Apparently, he represented only 25 male models and worked very closely with each. I felt honored to be there.

We then sat down as he very slowly paged through my book of

19

photos that the Paris agencies had recently preened so only my last and best test photos were still in it. Every now and then, he looked up and at me in a knowing fashion. He asked me to stand up—I did. He told me to turn around—I did. He then told me to take off my shirt so he could see my body. I blushed as my quickness in taking it off surprised me. I wanted to show that I was confident and unafraid in doing what he required to be his model. At his direction, I put my shirt back on and sat down. I was in.

I was to go back to my residence and freshen up and come back with my passport. We would supposedly have a photo test that same day with a wardrobe that was unparalleled by any other photographer in Milan. Hobbes said he knew all the top designers. I rushed back to my apartment, turned on the video recorder and recorded myself flipping through the pages of photos that my powerful booker had placed in my new book emblazoned with an exclusive UP insignia.

Upon my return to the agency, I found Hobbes to be less attentive. There was to be no photo shoot for that day, which left me hanging around the agency—an activity I later learned was typical, to let agents observe their new models, and for models to impress upon agents their desire to work. Unfortunately, superficial socializing had always been challenging for me unless I was buzzed. Nonetheless, I feigned friendliness with the other male models, who perched themselves on window ledges or were otherwise randomly draped around the room. Everyone, I seemed to notice, checked me, the new guy, out. Some simply said hello, some said nothing, and others asked questions that I felt reflected more on their desire to compete than to befriend. Their testosterone-laden gregariousness reminded me of the cocky, boisterous school boys whom I felt inhibited around. Yet there was a deeper rambunctiousness in their mockingly sensuous camaraderie. I conjectured it was an alluring sense of mystique that made them so appealing. More accurately, sexual confusion emanated from them and from me.

After what felt like hours later, I was sent to my first go-see, or visit to a potential client who might have a job at a future date. The agency asked if I had a map. I said, "no," which was simply responded to by "you better get one." That left me only the insufficient diagram I had taken from the hotel lobby. Deciding to introduce myself to Milano public transportation, I quickly found a trolley that I only guessed might take me in the right direction and from which I had no idea where to debark. My sweaty and confused look brought smiles from the other passengers, who made me curious; were they looking at me because I looked like a model?—I had a book after all. Or, did they wonder how this silly, confused tourist landed so far away from the normal sights? I waffled between self-consciousness and self-importance. Finally, I summoned the humility to ask a fellow passenger for some idea of my direction. Soon others joined in with a response, and together they got me off the trolley and miraculously onto the right street.

Once at the potential client's, I patiently sat in the waiting room. Waiting with me was another of Hobbes' models—a forty-something, handsome, yet somewhat puffy-looking man named Wade. Wade had been a Marlboro Man (so he said) and was back in town from Los Angeles to freshen up his book. Indeed, his book was as thick as the Parisian agencies warned me they could be. But most of the photos were of a much younger Wade. In fact just about all of them were. Seemingly, he had made a fortune with his shoots taken at the pinnacle of classic male modeling in the nineteen eighties.

Wade went in first, exited, and quickly popped into a waiting cab. My meeting was cordial but quick, for it didn't take long to go through my entire book of nine photos. After the casting, I sprung for a cab just as the older model had, and returned to the agency. They sent me to make photocopies of pictures that would make up my first card. Although the cost for these was minimal, I was already approaching zero dollars left from my initially available cash. But I was a model and living in the fashion capital of the world—or so I believed. To celebrate my successful day, I guiltily proceeded to drink what I told my camcorder had only been a half bottle of wine as I wrote in my journal and recorded myself blabbering drunkenly about fashion mongers.

Journal, June 3: *I was really shocked; a combination between utter surprise, disbelief, and ecxtasy. This is it. Somehow I still entertained the rest of the day in a state of disbelief. I felt like the same old HP Bob in a facade and just playacting as if I were paying for this experience as part of a neat, fancy vacation package set up by the travel agencies. But really, it is possible, it is happening, it is real? I am writing this after spending the whole day at the agency watching people motor in and out - other models - part of an elite Fraternity in which I am a member. Finally getting accepted to the fraternity. The Tres swank Fraternity of Ugly People! If I need to I will use my retirement savings. Who needs to worry about this for the next 30 years anyway? There is no turning back now. I am so happy inside. INSIDE. Not the wine speaking. I know I would be happy without the wine.*

Returning to the agency the next day for the ever-elusive, yet once more postponed photo-test, I found myself sent off to another go-see. There I saw Wade once again. This time, an elderly client who I thought was an editor for Vogue invited both of us into his small office. The man looked through Wade's pre-bloated tear sheets with great interest, all the while making comments on the extent of Wade's fine and former career. He then flipped through mine so quickly I could feel a breeze. Afterward, Wade invited me to a restaurant. I agreed, and he paid for the taxi. Together we sat at a table in a wonderful, sunny outdoor cafe with a veranda. A young model named Lothar, who Wade knew and would soon become my first roommate and friend, joined us. We then all proceeded to drink a shot of Italian grappa and a couple of beers—a lethal combination.

After lunch, Lothar and I recklessly crashed Wade's high-level perfume casting—not a highly favorable thing to do, either for the client or Hobbes (who luckily had a more relaxed attitude about this than any other booker did). Continuing to make the day into a festive summertime event, Wade sprung for more grappa and beers at another wonderful outdoor piazza restaurant/bar. During the conversation that ensued, Wade frankly asked me if I were gay (I later recorded the retelling of the entire scene and what followed in both videos and my written journal). Shocked and horrified that he would ask me such a thing, I replied that I wasn't. He replied that it seemed odd, because "he would have taken me for one."

I had always been sexually interested and emotionally in love with men. In my youngest years, I would occasionally become erect from being close to or looking at a sexy man's chest, or during other random occurrences (gym locker rooms, wrestling with a neighbor boy). Conversely, I deeply empathized with girls' (and women's) longings and their passions of the heart. One of the reasons I favored female friendships was because I felt self-conscious in the company of men. Pointless seductions by college girls had failed, however. When I once decided to take the initiative, a college co-ed friend, who allowed me to squish her boobs, ended up giggling, putting on her bra, and returning to her own room.

I mostly played the happy-go-lucky pothead, party-guy in college and beyond, and it helped avoid questions and obfuscate my true desires with men. But by the end of graduate school, most of my friends had moved on or coupled off, leaving me alone—my grandmother's high-school affirmation that I was just waiting for the right girl had long ago lost its believability. Desperate for human touch, while living with a group of friends as I started my employ with HP, I condescended to allow a woman, who would eventually become my first girlfriend, to fuck herself on me—her ex-boyfriend coincidentally was a male model. I was relieved that I was "normal" and gleeful when a month later she decided she had to make a permanent move out of state. I spent the next five years leading up to this trip unsuccessfully dating women. During those years, I had two sexual experiences with men: full sexual intercourse with a male fraternity brother (a year after my first girlfriend fled) and a blowjob from my newest male drinking buddy just before my "vacation." Despite how natural, exciting, or rewarding the experiences were for me, I disregarded them as drunken flings.

One experience above them all was the most challenging to refute. Two years before leaving for Europe, I was once again horny for a man I considered my best friend—Petey. In fact, I truly believed I was in love with him. This time, my feelings, consistent hard-ons, and masturbatory thoughts were undeniable. I could no longer pretend that I wasn't at least part gay. I dreamt that if I admitted this to him he would also come out and we could live in domestic bliss. I told my mother, grandmother, friends, and made a tape recording of my thoughts. Finally, while speaking with him on the phone and unable to express my newfound honesty, he asked me, "Robert, are you gay?" "Yes," I replied before shyly asking him. "No," he said simply, "but it's cool if you are." His easy reply destroyed me.

Hadn't we spent every weekend together, sometimes sleeping in our underwear in my waterbed, once with our knees slightly touching to the point where neither of us slept a wink, although we both pretended to? Hadn't he said first, "I love you, Bert" (the nickname he called me)? Shattered, I retreated and prayed to God that I would never again have homosexual thoughts or feelings. I then reneged my former coming out to my family, who were quite honestly relieved, and friends—none of whom were gay or knew how to handle the situation or help me accept myself. I diligently blamed my feelings, physical arousal, and coming out on my newly realized alcoholism.

In Milan, as lunch progressed, Wade proceeded to tell me that our agent, Hobbes, would soon surely invite me, the new boy, to the beachside chateau of a friend for testing. There, as evening fell, he would try to fuck me—I imagined a big orgy of men in which each had to succumb to the insatiable appetite of our old, overweight booker. If I were to refuse, he continued, I would be shunned, not sent to castings, and I would probably get little work. If I chose to go along with it, I risked exposure. Also, I feared, I would be selling my soul to the devil.

Later that afternoon, as I returned to the agency, Hobbes did exactly as Wade said he would. He invited me away for the weekend to a beautiful seaside mansion where I and three other boys would be tested free; it would save us the normal $150 fee we would otherwise have to pay another test photographer. Wade was right. I immediately panicked. Still buzzed from lunch, I blurted out, "Hobbes, I'm not gay." Stunned, Hobbes escorted me into the back room, followed by Antonella. He informed me that he had been trying to contact me all afternoon. In turn, I told him that I had been hanging out (drinking) with Wade and going to (crashing) his castings. Luckily, Hobbes let this pass as he proceeded to scold me: "What you do from 6 p.m. until 9 a.m. is your business…I invited you to a casting and you tell me you're not gay. What am I supposed to think? If you tell that to a client, what do you think they'll say?" he continued quite angrily. "There's a time and a place for that," he concluded.

Feeling mortified that I had created a scene of disastrous proportions where there may not have been any sinister intentions—other models later told me that sexual exploitation wasn't the truth—I shifted into survival mode. The agency was my only hope for a future. It was, from my perspective, my salvation from a numbingly isolating, inane, and empty prior existence. I apologized profusely, which I later chastised myself for. Antonella witnessed the entire communication and asked Hobbes to give me another chance. Respecting her voice, he relented. I was still in. Upon my return to my hotel room, I threw my shirt off and recorded the episode in my camcorder as follows:

Video Friday, June 4: *Oh Gahahahahahahddddddd - what's his name, Wade tells me he thinks I'm gay, thought I was gay, he's taken me for gay. What Hobbes normally does is he tries to get up their fucking butt and then… I see Hobbes and he says 'I get you photography for free'…I said, 'I'm not gay.' He freaks - He fucking freaks on me…It's the end of my modeling. It's all over. It's all over. He wanted to FUCKING end it RIGHT there. WELL FUCK. FUCK. Better end it now then on some fucking retreat and I get fucked by him. And then what? Then where do we go? I need to know what's going on. I'm going to quit my job, and it's leading me nowhere to an early grave, and I'm working over here in* *the middle of Milan, in the middle of fucking Milan. You know I don't have any money yet. I sat around the agency for six hours yesterday. Is he going to send me on castings? Fuck, I've got to stop being so nervous. What's going on? Everyone thinks I'm gay. It has nothing to do with sexual preference. Ha - it has everything to do with sexual preference.*

While I continued to gulp wine in the midst of my rancor, Lothar called me and invited me away for the weekend—apparently, he knew of parties outside the city. We'd have to take a train, but I was ready. "Just bring a shirt and fuck the comb," I recorded myself saying to Lothar while on the phone. The trip ended up falling through. Instead I spent the weekend partying with him at the *Residencia Giusti*, a building reserved specifically for models that would soon become my home, and at clubs (Hollywood's, Club L.A., and Lizards) that would lead to many models' ruin. I concluded my first full weekend as a model in Milan writing the following in my journal:

Journal Sunday, June 6: *A lifetime away from my last writing. I am in another stratosphere, another world…My mind has sunk to the mind of a vegetable. Smoking Pakistani hash and it's Africa hot here in Milan. I've had a couple of crisis of the heart and some ball building experiences… I haven't yet even quit my job…. I'm worried. I'm concerned. I can only have hope that if I cut myself off completely somehow I will survive. God's will be with me. I can't go back to HP. I can't go back to California yet. It's just not in the cards… Now the next major concern. I have been raging all weekend. At the clubs of Milan…For Free…drinks, discounts on food, everything – because WE ARE MODELS. This is a concept I need to fully and soberly absorb, realize and SELF ACTUALIZE to.*

Wade said he would have taken me for gay (twice). This hurt deep down, because it's so true from what I have experienced all my life from others and also from my own feelings at times. It sets me off into a vicious cycle of self-doubt, and lowered self-esteem. I've felt it all weekend and today. I question my looks, my goals, my potential, my laugh, mannerisms, lifestyle, thoughts and actions. Especially, this in tangent with quite a bit of partying and, viola, I fall back into the self-defeating little mole I had become before venturing on my full recovery program. I need to give

26

up control, practice honesty and handle each day one day at a time. I don't feel as stereotyped. Although I do feel like some sort of image. Something to be looked at.

Last night I spent dancing with a beautiful 18-year-old Swedish girl. I danced with the thought in my mind of not getting carried away. Of thinking of her as unapproachable. We danced for hours as if we were in a photo shoot and everyone was looking at us and everyone WAS! I kept trying to portray the expression that I was indifferent to her. That I could have women like her and that I have had women like her in the clique of my fingers. That I was numb, confident, and only slightly interested.

Her eyes were so beautiful. I felt as if I should melt in there. That keeping up such a front was futile. But I kept it up. We kept getting closer. Our lips nearly touching and then moving away. She touching me. I her. She putting her hands up and down my body in my pants and under my shirt. I had several actual erections. I tried not to bother her with. We finally started to and did make out in the middle of the dance floor. Going around and around and around to the beating sounds of the American music and the flashing colors of the surrounding lights. It was magnificent. It was one of the most memorable experiences I should ever have in my life. It was fun. We continued to kiss at the entrance to her residence until I opened the door for her to let her in at 5:30 AM. At least I've learnt something and it seems to have worked.

And it can and will work with everything in my life. This subtle indifference. This utter lack of concern with money or human companionship or love. I need to realize that I can give and be open but don't need to receive this. Not really want I need to express a self-glowing confidence that I have all the emotional and financial security that I need to go through life as a happy and healthy human being. This is what everyone wants to see.

Lothar taught me something last night also. He taught me when we started at each other directly at the forehead between the eyes to open up completely. To open any secrets of my soul and make them visible. I thought that I have no secrets. That I have opened up anything that can ever be thought of as a secret to somebody, to God, to myself. I felt open and experienced the same sort of deep morose that I had...I showed that to him. He asked if I felt the energy. I did.

Ugly People 04

Having proved myself as one of the guys over the weekend, I accepted Lothar's invitation to become his roommate at the Residencia Giusti first thing Monday afternoon (June 7). This would save me from spending far beyond what I could afford on a hotel and place me in the middle of the hotspot of model life. The Giusti (pronounced "Juice-Tea") was a large, affordable residence strictly for models that looked and functioned very much like a college dormitory. Each room had it's own bathroom and a small kitchen and most had two pull out sofas that transformed into mildly comfortable beds.

I felt comfortable sharing this small but efficient space with Lothar because, unlike some of the other boys I would soon meet and befriend, he was neither cocky nor overwhelmingly sexy. He was safe and reminded me of the kind of guys I used to hang out and party with. Lothar was from Hamburg and shortly would return to his apartment there, leaving me alone in my new room having to pay only half the rent. When he returned he moved in with Zoë, his Swedish model girlfriend he had met a year before when she was 17. Zoë was a successful model. Concerning Lothar's career in modeling, she hoped for the best, but being a realist, she cooperated with his parents to advise Lothar to go back to school, settle down, party less, and start a family. Lothar wasn't quite ready for this yet, wanting instead to earn a million dollars so he could then retire. He had a long way to go since he had only one successful modeling campaign during the entire time I knew him, which he had completed two years previously in Tokyo.

My mood in the Giusti was enthusiastic and cheerful. I had always loved the dorms and college and was still living under the delusion that the party I experienced there was never ending. Here, once again, I was placed in a setting in which beautiful young men and women (who were many times teenage girls) would be partying all through the night any night of the week. My journal entry that day reflected my newly confident and delusional thinking that I would "easily out-model many of the other bozos." I would also gain a "sober, comfortable rhythm to my life of exercise, water, activity, yoga, prayer, writing, reading and thinking," which I thought were the reasons I had to stay at HP for so long—none of this was to occur regularly.

Within my first day at the Giusti I met a woman who would become one of my best friends. Originally from Vancouver, Aurora was 26, considered old for a female model, and had worked for ten years. When I met her she was both savvy and bitter about the modeling industry and a chronic hash smoker. It was through her that I established my first connection to purchase hash, which allowed me to behave as I had in college and immediately become a daily, many-times-a-day smoker. I immensely enjoyed watching her roll a joint using her long, beautiful fingers to break open a cigarette (she also was a hand, leg, and foot model). She would spread its tobacco on a cigarette paper, soften a rock of hash with a lighter, crumble it on the tobacco, and then, with a quick, efficient flourish, roll the entire concoction into a perfectly stylized joint that she would lift to her pretty lips and inhale with all the grace of Katherine Hepburn or Betty Davis. This act alone, so similar to a debonair, slightly-older girl who taught me how to enjoy pot during my first year in college, made me want her as a friend.

At first, I relished the hours and days we spent together smoking hash cigarettes and talking. Mostly I listened to her talk about men—a fact I eventually grew deeply resentful of and secretly (in my journals) blamed for my inability to seduce her. Emasculated by my inability to be open about my own feelings towards men, I felt as sexless and speechless as I had when listening to my mother involve me—her only child—in matters concerning my father's infidelities, which were equally fraught with tension and too big for me to handle.

Soon I knew of Aurora's love history and heard her frustrations. Lost at love, yet always yearning for it, she was a little girl badly hurt. And she was constantly looking for a sensitive straight male touch to help her heal, and most likely a good gay friend to listen. Unfortunately, she was attracted to men who treated her poorly.

Aurora continually complained about living in the pit she considered Milan to be, yet consistently came back because she found it the best and most affordable place to get good tests and editorial photos that maintained her modeling "day-rate" in her home base of Hamburg. She still had hope that she would eventually have greater success. Through her, I got a sense of how the industry worked, where I needed to earn money (the U.S., Germany, possibly Paris) and what I needed to get there (tear sheets or tests from Milan, or if I was lucky, Paris). She also taught me how to live as a model in other ways too. She instructed me how to make an incredible, affordable salad out of lettuce, beets, garlic, garbanzo beans, tomatoes, and olive oil. We prepared a perfect espresso using a little metal espresso maker that came with our rooms, with just the right amount of creamy whole milk. She taught me how to wash my clothes in the bathtub. I had unfortunately learned the hard way the first time by adding my red shirt to the mix, and thereby ruining all of my clothes except for the black ones. Luckily black was in that season.

Life in Milan became more comfortable in other ways too. My relationship with Hobbes had patched up enough that he told me that he was going to send me to Armani—in fact, he said he was going to send me everywhere except for Versace (who "liked big men and would treat me very badly"). Hanging over this potentially new and fascinating life was one major decision I still had to make. My original flight was scheduled to depart in two days, and the time had come for me to make the call to Hewlett-Packard. I still had options, one of which was to ask for a leave of absence, which would give me several extra months of time off. But this ordinarily had to be requested in advance and was only given to über-important engineers. So I had to

30

either call and quit or plan on packing my things and leave the very next day.

I believed that I would have to leave HP (or any other situation, location, or person) before I could fully move into my passion. That while I was still enslaved to the "Master Corporation," I suffered too much to be able to have the strength or clarity to move on. Many a day, after slogging on a spreadsheet at a computer, I found a need to decompress—which in my case meant hard-core surfing, dope, and alcohol to both enliven and numb me down—before I could regain the energy it took to find new solutions or act on them. Decompressing often ended up taking so long that I was stuck, having made no progress on my goals to get out. Therefore, in order for real change to occur, I believed I needed to place all of my material self-worth, ownerships, and obligations at risk, and, with luck, persistence, self-belief, and appropriate timing, make a dramatic change.

Alone in my room that afternoon, Tuesday, June 8, I turned my video camera on my shirtless body as I got on my knees on the hard linoleum floor, put my elbows on the bed next to the mini-refrigerator that served as the phone table and prayed the Lord's Prayer and asked God for guidance. I picked up the phone and began to dial. I had hoped to call my own work number and erase any personal messages I had, but found out I couldn't since the phone in Milan was a huge, old fashioned, dial phone and I would have required a push button to follow my plan. Frustrated, I thought this was a bad sign. Maybe I should go back; I hesitated.

Realizing again that this was the hardest decision I had ever made in my life, I decided to call my manager and tell him I was taking a leave of absence. I called the main switchboard operator instead of his number. The woman who answered was a lovely British woman who had worked the switchboard for a long time and knew of me from a number of suppliers who had called during the years. "Good morning, this is Robert Reincke calling from overseas," I said, and laughed as she recognized me. "Promise not to tell anyone, but I'm in

Milan," I told her, before I had the idea that she could help me make my decision. "You know what I'm trying to do? This is a very difficult decision. You have to help me, okay? I've come to Milan to become a model. And I got signed by an agency. And I'm on vacation from work and my vacation ends tomorrow. So now I have to decide whether or not to quit or get a 20-day leave of absence, or what," I questioned hungrily.

Within milliseconds I responded, "Quit…Yeah?…Just do it… Ha? Yeah. And forget about the 20-day leave of absence and all that crap," as I felt my bare chest with my free hand. "Just say 'hey I gotta quit,'" I laughed. Finally, someone heard. For the first time in my life someone understood me and encouraged me to live my dreams. The phone system operator at Hewlett-Packard had become the parent I always wanted. She continued to tell me that one had to live one's dreams and explore Europe and the world when one still could. That she moved to another country and never regretted it and would do it all over again if she were younger. We spent the next several minutes transferring into and out of humanless voicemail systems of one manager after the other who were not there. I finally ended up leaving a message in the Human Resources Department manager's voicemail box instructing her to mail my last check and any other information to my mother. I agreed to send the operator a picture of my first published shot, which I never did, and hung up the phone.

I was officially a model, I concluded, as my head fell onto my shoulder in utter comfort and the overwhelming feeling that everything would be all right. I would have some fun in my life doing something that was enjoyable. The decision was handed to me, and I felt, for that moment, completely serene in the knowledge of it. I immediately recorded the event in my journal with a little poem expressing that I felt "free and exhausted as if years of shackles were falling off my back…and then ate a salami sandwich." I was "on my way." It would be "Milan and Paris for a year and then the shows and New York. I will be 30." And then, I felt anxious again.

With the umbilical cord cut, my fragile sense of self was immediately challenged the next day. What started as a simple haircut in preparation for my first Milanese test photo shoot turned into much more. For all of my life prior to becoming a model I had gotten a simple John F. Kennedy-style barber cut—short and parted on the side. It wasn't until I started having photo shoots that I went to a stylist in San Diego, who was a straight guy with a girlfriend that made me feel comfortable. Speranze, the stylist I met in Milan, was a completely different experience. Feeling like a little boy at his first haircut, I nervously sat in the chair and answered his eager questions about my new life as a model. After finishing with the cut, he suggested that many male models actually had their pubic hairs cut so that if they got a job in a bathing suit, they would be ready. I considered this reasonable and agreed to go with him to the back of the salon. There on a massage table surrounded by curtains, he instructed me to take off all my clothes and lay under the blanket. After he returned he nervously took the electric clippers to my crotch, delicately moving my penis from side to side. Having had very little physical contact throughout my life, the episode resulted in my immediate and thorough excitation. Sweating profusely, he continued to do the best he could until a female coworker walked into the area and interrupted our progress. The look she gave made me realize that this was highly unusual for this upscale boutique, just feet away from matronly women getting their hair done. I left thoroughly embarrassed and feeling violated.

Returning to my residence, I then met a gorgeous male who would become an acquaintance and future roommate. No matter what Trent, a New York Boss model, wore, he looked sexy. One could find him sauntering about the residence in a sleeveless, plaid flannel shirt, worn unbuttoned to reveal his perfect, hard abs and well-defined, bronze chest, with his black and white New York Yankees baseball cap on, or tussled back, nicely cropped hair. No matter how fucked-up he got, he had a sparkle in his dark eyes and smile on his sultry lips, revealing his perfect white teeth. He knew he was hot and how to use it, which was very different from most men I had ever known.

That evening and a couple nights later, Trent took the effort to make me dinners—oil and garlic and vegetarian pastas. In the past I thoroughly enjoyed my male friends who felt comfortable enough hanging out with me to share their intimate feelings, hopes, dreams, and relationships. I sometimes got hard-ons while alone, late at night, talking to my best college buddies (two in particular). But since the episodes were always surrounded by pot, I thought my reaction could be explained as an aberration and dismissed it. It eventually went away as I continued to smoke and focus my mind on something else.

Evenings in which Trent and I hung out also confused me. His attentions seemed to border on the flirtatious, which he combined with a great deal of sexual innuendo. Flirting felt compromising, and I never quite understood male locker-room banter, a form of flirtatious teasing that men could seemingly get away with. None of my regular, non-jock male friends participated in this. I occasionally felt giddy feelings (even when they didn't include a hard-on), blushed, or smiled awkwardly when I saw a man who was not only attractive, but also moved me. I never knew how to understand this and often looked quickly away in shame. I had no idea how to behave in the presence of such a naturally seductive man as Trent. I smoked a lot, drank more, and after our first dinner, spent the rest of that night traipsing around the Giusti meeting, chatting, and partying with random groups of girls, much as I had in the dormitories or my fraternity at Michigan State University.

The following day I worked out in the gym before my first test photo shoot in Milan. The photographer seemed a genuine, regular person and took some good pictures of me wearing much of my own wardrobe and some that I had borrowed from others. Feeling comfortable, I continued to use the tricks I had learned to make pictures turn out well (I clenched my jaw, lifted my upper eyelid, and kept my lips relaxed) while he productively insisted that I continue to relax. The resulting photos successfully captured the playful, sexual naiveté that at least my subconscious was experiencing. That night, feeling sensually enlivened, arrogantly proud, and emotionally fraught from the shoot, I hit the clubs with my new friends Trent and Aurora.

We started at a club appropriately named Hollywood's (a dive bar that tried to impart a facade of glamour and privilege) and then headed to another equally telling bar called Tutti Frutti. There bubbles pumped onto the dance floor and sometimes submerged shirtless male dancers under a foamy brew which hid indiscretions. I drank an excessive amount to further obscure what was happening. I eventually found myself being encouraged by a table of men to dance in the foam alone, where I ruined my one pair of black leather wingtips.

The next day, Trent kindly took me shoe shopping, where I found a replacement pair far more appropriate for my new circumstances. Instead of wingtips, I bought a pair of boot-type black leather shoes that had an inscription of the Western Hemisphere on the sole (symbolic of my adventures into the new, international world of modeling). Bathing me in brotherly affections, Trent bought me a shot of Jaegermeister and then took me to the park where he introduced me to the Hare Krishna from whom I could buy pot, thereby relieving my sole dependency on Aurora. Upon our return to my new home, I very happily video taped Aurora draped in airy clothes with my new shoes on her feet and Trent making his customary, confusing, sexual comments. I later boldly threw my old pair of soiled wingtips in the garbage. Discarding shoes would become a ritual I continued for the rest of my life whenever I made a cataclysmic or dramatic change.

The taping continued as we got higher and higher well into the evening, Trent teased, and we joined Aurora in her apartment where she, too, cooed and flirted with her sensual, blond roommate Electra. The twosomes of Aurora and Electra, Trent and I were heading out for my second night in a row to all the big discos of Milan. I made one last jerky motion with the camcorder from what seemed like Aurora flicking Electra's tit to Trent saying something that I didn't understand. I interrupted everyone, turned the camcorder to my face, and claimed that "we were all true Generation X's," which made no sense (since they all considered me a wealthy, American Yuppie). I began guffawing in guttural, stifled, unnatural and terrifically sarcastic laughter that would make my friends roll on the floor screaming at the sound of it. I had arrived—the new, asexual lush of the model residence—just as I had in the dormitories twelve years before. The differences, however, were many, not the least of which was that I soon would need to support myself.

Fishtailing 05

I had my second photo test within a week of my first. The second photographer was a young, handsome black man, who allowed me to sort through his wardrobe in an effort to choose a good selection of clothing. After I put on one of his V-neck, tight-fitting sweaters without a shirt on underneath, he put one hand on each of my shoulders and gently pushed them down and back. In a soft, comforting voice, he asked me if I had ever been teased in high school. He explained that by crunching my shoulders forward as I had, I was protecting myself from childhood or teenage taunting. I later wrote "I confessed to him all of my homosexual acts to that time," which might have included the two boys I'd had sex with. As the day progressed and the sun sank, we shot at the site of what apparently was the historical grounds of a church. I later described "…green grass, beautiful trees and decaying stone structures. On the wall to my left a painted Ying and Yang sign and a sculpture of some sort of a Saint in the garden." We smoked hash, as I fought my paranoid feelings and tried to feel tantalized by the appropriate, sexy, preppy look he was going for.

After the shoot, I bought myself a cross and then returned to my apartment where I video recorded myself slowly unbuttoning and then taking off my black linen shirt, flicking my hair back, and then unbuttoning and re-buttoning the top two buttons of my black jeans. I told the camera that "today I totally opened myself up sexually for the first and only time that I need to or am going to…the photographer is just hoping to get the pictures and jack off on them…this doesn't mean I need to be confused about my sexuality though…after all, I am open about it." "What a nightmare to have to fishtail about my sexuality in this industry of sexual deviants," I also wrote, "…all I want is to be famous." Despite this I spent the following days obsessively worried about my shoulders and tried to hold them back so no one else could see what he had.

Straight talk and tough acting crescendoed as an onslaught of male models came to Milan for the spring shows. Thousands descended upon the city from the United States and from many other countries. Castings increased to several a day and on the weekend. The Giusti swelled to capacity with men from all over the world as the tone became boisterous and macho. I tried to comply with the heightened straight-acting and belligerent vibe to the best of my ability. In my private journals I convinced myself that I was in love with Aurora. After coming home from late night partying at Hollywood's bar I secretly bragged to my camcorder about hanging out with a black female prostitute, perhaps to regain my heterosexual status after it had been unbalanced by interactions with both my gay, black booker and photographer.

Soon after, another incredibly sexy, blond, blue-eyed man named Rusty entered my world. Like Aurora, Rusty was Canadian and interested in books, which I perceived as non-threatening and pleasant. Like Trent he seemed to immediately identify me as a yuppie, which he obviously appreciated. Confusingly, he also occasionally exhibited the flirtatious, sexual undertones that I had experienced with Trent—he showed me his abs while he winked flirtatiously and jokingly played with my upper thighs under the table when an unusually voluptuous British woman and her twiggy-type peers video recorded a drunken dinner party he held for us. I didn't know nor thought to question if Rusty was gay, just as I hadn't Trent or anyone else. I just assumed everyone must be straight. No one talked about being gay, bi, or questioning, either, and all treated the one man in the residence who everyone knew was openly gay as a pariah. I much later learned that contrary to prior times, fashion designers (many of whom were still in the closet) had grown to favor straight and straight-acting male models. In response, whenever a male model came to Milan he acted straight regardless of his sexuality. To a fault, while AIDS was killing more gay men than at

38

any other time in history, in Milan that season and the season to come, it also supposedly didn't exist. This huge information gap enhanced the insanity I constantly felt.

Two weeks after my arrival, I worked my first job—*Max*, one of the top fashion, style, and pop magazines in Europe. I was one of several models who each got one page and one change of clothing in an editorial that featured fashionable clothes from top Italian designers. The other models were some of the biggest up-and-coming male models in the world—one of whom soon became a new roommate. This outstanding opportunity legitimized my career for me, but unfortunately paid nearly nothing—$60, of which the agency took its standard (for Italy) 40% fee. Yet this was common for good editorial or fashion show jobs where the pretence for paying badly was that the model could use the pictures to get better, higher paying jobs.

I showed up to work without a hangover, well rested, alert as I could be with the significant build-up of TCH from hash always present in my system, and on-time. I pretended—as I did when I finally had sex as a 24-year-old—that this was not the first time. I was dressed in a business suit designed by Kirzauomo with pants that unfortunately were so long they had to be pulled up on my stomach like Fred Mertz wore in episodes of *I Love Lucy* (most likely due to the fact that the height we put on my comp card represented me as taller than I was). My hair was styled, my generally good complexion slightly powdered, and I was told how to pose by the photographer, who, in his professionalism, left no detail unattended. Following his directions was easy. He took a Polaroid to devise the set-up, which he later gave me, and quickly completed the task.

As I left, the adrenalin rush I had been experiencing subsided, and I reverted to my usual feelings of inadequacy. Feeling good about the job but dissatisfied about me, I questioned why no one talked to me. What a lonely job, I thought, when no one questions a single thing about you. I wrote in my journal that I was overwhelmed, acknowledged that I had "entered party phase II of my life," wanted to "smoke hash and drink, and needed to stop." Nonetheless, feeling strangely lonely, empty, and hollow inside, I still numbed myself by spending some time thereafter getting high with Trent, who confusingly was fooling around with some girl.

The next several days I went on castings for Valentino, Katharine Hamnett, Barbati, Byblos, Franco Pagetti, Inghirami, Basile, Fugiwara, and others. The mass of male models and intensity of activities were beyond my capacity to fully absorb. Agencies from Paris and the rest of the world were also in town to recruit models for their countries. I continually dumbed-down my intellect with a farcical, bland, social exterior that I had used as a survival technique in Michigan as each new male acquaintance entered into Aurora and my lives. The only intelligent talk was the consistent drone of insecurity that surrounded the weeding out of models due to the capricious nature of fashion. No one knew exactly what the fashion designers wanted since they kept their inspirations secret to the last minute. I worried that I had made a horrendous mistake by cutting my long hair before I went to Europe, when a brigade of long-haired male models set up residency at the Giusti. When long hair appeared to be out that season, they all had to consider whether or not they should cut their hair in time to quickly reposition themselves with new test photographs for the Paris shows that followed. Word of mouth, the only source of vital information that may affect the livelihood of any model, was correct that season, and in Paris longhairs were *in*. I was happy to not have had to consider those decisions. And even happier when I found out that I had obtained the largest, most spectacular show of the season—the Hugo Boss show—that would be in Cologne, Germany in several weeks.

With the shows over, many of the testosterone-laden men, Rusty, and my latest top-model roommate from New York, left. With nowhere else to go, I remained, hoping to make money to pay back the Visa that I had been taking cash advances from, to get some more tests with the good photographers that were still in town, and to finally get my long-promised, free, nicely-suited test with Hobbes. Remaining in Milan during this time was rumored to be a potentially beneficial strategy. Castings continued, and my odds of getting work were supposedly improving since so many of the competitive male models were leaving for the shows in Paris and New York and many more were going home in preparation for the big summer slowdown and August shutdown (the agencies in Milan and Paris were closed during the entire month of August). Others were still coming, including a new roommate, Rudi, who were aware of this strategy.

Journal July 1: *The hoopla is now over. The shows are in Paris next week and all the hopefuls and rising stars that have survived and endured Milan for the past weeks and months have left; leaving newcomers and yet still hopefuls but not yet quite ready for Paris types such as myself behind. Me, I just decided to learn my jacket size today. After all this time, and after yet another humiliating experience at a casting where they actually really seemed to like me and then lost it all when I couldn't tell the woman my simple jacket size. I feel so stupid. So bad. Why does it take me so long to figure this simple thing out? Katerina at Glamour was right. If I were in Paris I would be run over by the guys with the big books, big names, big experiences, big tear-sheets, possibly become very frustrated, very poor, and never want to come back to Paris again. I am not Bob or Robert the buyer anymore. I am Robert Reincke the model. I am a serious mature man pursuing my career in MODELING.*

With many of his more prestigious models in Paris or gone, Hobbes finally supposedly had more time for me. My test with him was rescheduled for the first week in July, shortly after the shows ended. It seemed such a sure thing that he gave me his personal home phone number. By the end of that Friday, nothing had yet to be confirmed for Saturday. Partly in response, I drank so heavily with Lothar that I puked—something I rarely did. Horribly hung-over, I obsessively called Hobbes all day Saturday; even though I truly hoped by then he wouldn't be available. He wasn't. By Sunday (America's Independence Day), recovered from my hangover, I maintained a hash buzz while waiting for the phone to ring. Hobbes was out of town, I later learned. Discouraged, within a couple days I took a photo shoot with another (my third) Milanese test photographer, whose crisp, clean, conservative images were good, but disfavored by Hobbes.

That week, Aurora left to go back to her apartment she had spoken of so glowingly in contrast to the Giusti. Despite the fact that I would be staying with her in a couple weeks and we had only known each other for a month, I felt an overwhelming sense of sadness and loss—not necessarily for Aurora but for what she meant to me. Aurora reminded me of a friend from college—Linda—whom I had also known for a short period, and likewise considered an amazingly elegant, sophisticated woman.

Linda also initiated me into a new phase of my life and simultaneously introduced me to concepts that would influence me for years. She was older than I and worldlier. She dressed with an expensive sensibility that made the well-dressed (preppy) elite look preposterous, and carried herself with a panache they didn't have the wherewithal to mimic. With her came an opening to the soul-searching and spiritual influences of the seventies—the decade prior to my collegiate experience, which I knew about, but were contrary to the more vulgar, surface realities I remembered. It was through her that I was introduced to Cat Stevens, Jethro Tull, Carol King and other soulful performers I had heard in the background of my youth, and on the stereo of my recent sexual tryst in Paris. She read books like *Jonathan Livingston Seagull*, *The Prophet* (which was a favorite of my mother's) and *The Road Less Traveled*, which Aurora also recommended. It was she who, for a moment, humored my drunken fondling of her breasts (perhaps to determine for herself if I was gay); and who took me along with her roommate to an MSU campus showing of the porn classic double feature of *Debbie Does Dallas* and *Deepthroat* (we all left laughing). Unfortunately it was also with her that I learned to love smoking pot, associating a bohemian sophistication with the experience and the privileged comfort she represented to me.

When Linda spontaneously decided to return to her native Connecticut and drop out of MSU in the middle of a too-harsh winter,

I felt she was abandoning me. After all that I had experienced through her, I didn't want her to leave. I knew there was so much more to learn and felt a strong attachment to her for caring about the real me—even before I knew who the real me was. My last memory of her was watching the dormitory elevator door close as I curtly and with great detachment looked at her briefly and snapped "Bye...see you later." I would not let this lugubrious goodbye repeat with Aurora, who would be the first woman of my modeling adventure I connected to these memories, which by then had morphed into what I mistakenly thought was sexual love. I video recorded (or had her roommate video record) every minute of our last interactions as she bitched-out the residence management over a conflict involving a joint burn in a blanket. Then I helped lug her baggage to a waiting cab.

As a chilly drizzle fell the night of her leaving, Lothar—who was one of the few models left—and I, participated in one of our most memorable moments together. Zoë was away, leaving him free to party heavier, devote his adventurous and creative instincts to me, and share conversation that he didn't with his girlfriend. After getting very high, Lothar mentioned that he knew of a cemetery nearby. He had once climbed up the ancient, ivy-covered, brick wall surrounding it and smoked a quiet joint there. I was intrigued with cemeteries, given an introduction to their coolness by Linda when she took me to the film *Harold and Maude*. The rain would make the entire experience more memorable we thought.

Off we went, laughing hysterically and inebriated down the hallway, chortling into the tiny red elevator, down to the first floor, out the door and into the drizzling night. Once there, having used a garbage bin to hop up the tall wall, Lothar walked at a fast pace. I kept my focus on my footing, not caring if I fell behind. Finally, we found a spot, sat down, and fondled the joint that he had wrapped in a bag in his pocket. We didn't smoke for long before one of us noticed it first. There below us, directly in front of the crematorium, was a man clad in what appeared to be black leather standing next to his equally dark motorcycle. Yet, we had heard no sound. And the door to the crematorium was bolted shut with a chain. Then we both saw the figure move. In horror we looked at each other briefly and then rushed away as quickly as we could. Getting down was quicker than getting up the wall, and we reveled in our experience until four in the morning.

Two days later—a week after my last failed attempt—was to be my big test with Hobbes. He had instructed me to make sure to get the rest I needed because he wanted to see my face relaxed and at ease. The day before, I drank and smoked with as much control as I could, video recording the room alone at night as the Carpenters played "Top of the World" in the background. The day of the shoot, I called him consistently but to no avail. I sat for hours in the sun in my favorite park, Sempione, with Lothar and a returned Zoë video recording our activities and an episode of fucking dogs (my mother and grandmother had taken me to see my grandmother's schnauzer fuck as an introduction to sex). By late afternoon, when I finally got the instruction to head over to Hobbes' apartment, my skin had begun to take on a red tone that matched my angry countenance.

To some degree I related to Hobbes as a dysfunctional father figure. I had always desperately wanted my father to support me for who I was and encourage my interests instead of those that society demanded. But being the Midwestern man he was, I felt us at odds as I chose art, piano, and theater to his preferred sports, mini-cycle riding, or go-cart building (all of which I participated in to some degree). With Hobbes, however, I felt a mutual understanding about a part of me that my father never verbally acknowledged.

I had always been aware of a manner of living that superseded that of being a Yuppie—that was, in fact, the lifestyle that yuppies had wanted to imitate by focusing on eating better foods, dressing in better-quality clothing, belonging to the right clubs or organizations, and drinking the right wines and beers. I was aware that there was a style of life that included privileges and amenities, sophistications and elegance, culture and traditions that made the upgrades of the baby boomer yuppies seem fraudulent. Perhaps it was from stories of my family's pre-Russian-Revolution wealth related to me by my aging grandmother: stories that I clung to in order to escape the bland and isolated existence I experienced in the Detroit suburbs of my youth. Or perhaps it was from the divas of the classic films I watched, whose melodramatic lives and yearnings for unrequited love I empathized with. In any case, I grew to appreciate all things classically elegant. In this regard, Hobbes had also piqued my interest from the very start with his promises of unobtainable, fine clothing and his understanding of how well they would suit me.

Nonetheless, as the sun, though fading, persistently clung to its bright heat, the heavy fall clothes that I wore became uncomfortable. My agitation prevented me from letting go of my distrust for Hobbes. I dramatically and mistakenly thought that older gay men like him represented a cruel and heartless gay agenda to recruit young and handsome youth such as me. Haunted by my emotional vulnerability, I found the shoot, which took place near a river and empty buildings in an obscure and unpopulated area in the outskirts of town, to be quite difficult. Even though I tried, I could not hold onto the regality that he and I knew I was capable of projecting. Hobbes demanded vociferously that I get into the mood. The more I tried to imagine being grand and noble, the more I felt disturbed and angry. We agreed to reconvene the following afternoon.

The next day, I had another photo shoot scheduled before Hobbes'. The photographer utilized my reddened features curiously as we shot in an abandoned iron works building by using elements of heat and fire to draw inspiration. It turned out to be the most entertaining, creative shoot I had experienced: a jacket I had borrowed was turned inside out and placed amidst many layers of other clothing; a pair of my shorts and a sweater were draped around my head as a make-shift turban; and I got the only chance I would ever get to wear the sexy, red pants I had bought in Paris.

Afterwards, once again late in the afternoon (Hobbes preferred the setting sun for shooting), we shot suits and ties as the light severely faded through the skylight in Hobbes' nicely appointed Milanese loft apartment. After it was over, I felt happily relieved that he and I saw eye-to-eye. I certainly had no reason to fear his advances, for he never once so much as initiated a sexual gesture. Hobbes, "who was no fool," taught me elegance and saw in me the ability to make my mark in a refined graceful manner and expensive, beautiful clothes. I later wrote of this with great satisfaction. As I celebrated what was to become the symbolic conclusion of my first time in Milan, the experience of what I defined as having "broke bread" with Hobbes, became so significant that I wrote, "I've felt my entire spirit has been lifted through my body, through a tunnel of light and joined the infinite united world of Love and God." I also wrote the following:

Journal July 13: *Hobbes says I'll do well. I believe him, but modeling is now a rich mans game. There are far fewer jobs and many more models. The old days of being treated like royalty are over. Today I almost felt like crying at my test. Hobbes was shooting me in beautiful clothes and I remembered being raised and wearing gorgeous outfits. Then he called me prissy – a grown homosexual man calling me prissy and I remembered the chastising I received as a child for being different, prissy or effeminate or a mommas boy. I wanted to cry because I was comfortable and looked darn good in the clothes I was wearing and as the person I am and I needn't be chastised again.*

My remaining ten days was unfettered by tests, castings, or jobs, leaving me free to party unencumbered by the bothersome obligation of work. I gleefully video recorded every detail of Lothar and I smoking hash out of a potato bong, while we drowned in an Absolut Citron punch concoction that he devised. A couple days later, I tried to "love the mosquitoes that attacked me in swarms as God's creatures as I sat underneath a canopy of green, velvet, trees, on a bench in the park," getting stoned with a despondent, filthy, and homeless Hare Krishna pot dealer, who had once been a beautiful female model—and who I described in my journal as "a woman deeply trying to find serenity and salvation from the horrible dreads of reality in a modern society." As the day changed to twilight and then night, "I confessed my belief faith in the Holy Ghost, Father and Jesus to her."

My last weekend, I spent at a seaside resort with my new roommate, Rudy, who was one of the other *Max* models and who I considered to be like a younger brother—"cool, sexually experienced, and with a perfect male body." We laid on the beach, his built body next to mine, and his hands cupping the wind as I toked endless joints, walked on the boardwalk, and spent evenings together smoking—he said he never smoked more pot in his life than he had with me. He too left for Hamburg where I would also briefly see him. However, despite video recording his departure as he walked down the hall into the elevator, I didn't feel the same sense of camaraderie I had with guys like Trent who I had spent less time with. Most likely because since Rudy was involved in a long-term relationship with a female model named Romy, I built our short-term friendship on inauthentic, macho rapport and straight-talking, Christian-sounding rhetoric.

Alone in the apartment, I met and fed another struggling, homeless, and hungry model girl named Godet, with whom I also smoked pot and watched and video recorded a freak summer hail storm. Again, feeling it was my calling to "pray for and save the Italian people" (and "the people of the world"), we talked about God and Christianity together as a rainbow appeared in the horizon. Godet explained that somewhere in the Bible God said, "and I will put a rainbow after every rainfall," which I recorded somewhat stupefied. She later ran away from the apartment of a photographer that I took her to (in a final effort to get rid of her). There I was gifted a large block of hash and she was apparently offered a massage (none of which I remember now, but recorded then).

As the end of my stay neared, I busied myself with work-related tasks too. I reviewed slides and proof sheets of my prior tests and worked with Hobbes to determine which to enlarge—he selected one or two from each of the four other photographers I had worked with and four from his shoots. I also made temporary cards and delivered

47

photos to a development facility to create new cards at a large expense, which I charged. Two days before I left Milan, Trent reappeared as my last roommate. The only other models that remained besides him were young girls and crazy British women. I had no energy left for these people. By then, I truly knew it was time to go.

I video recorded Trent one last time as he intonated in a flirty, drag-queen manner, "Hi I'm Trent," and pursed his lips. A young girl sitting in our room complained, "He's got that thing on constantly." I laughed—the only one left laughing—moved the camera to myself and said, "I've got to get me, the obnoxious," and stuck my tongue out. More alone than I knew, I was alienated from everyone who were equally alienated from themselves. I guffawed again for the last time in my camera and finally turned it off. I would shortly lose it and all its film after a drunken night following the Hugo Boss show.

During my last day I was told that I had obtained a $10,000 contract to live and work for two months in Tokyo for the highly reputable agency Team. I would quickly have to obtain a working visa while in Germany and would depart shortly after the Hugo Boss show. Interestingly, I would see Trent in Tokyo, but the memory of this is fleeting. We were never again to be as close as I imagined we were when we spent our playfully, intimate first weekend together sharing hash, shopping, and eating vegetarian pasta. Other guys would be just as temporary.

Two months after leaving the comforts, complications, and disappointments of my home in San Diego, I bought a plane ticket to Hamburg (to be reimbursed by the Hugo Boss people). Trent and I smoked all of my remaining pot, since I knew there would be plenty more with Aurora, and I wasn't confident about taking it on the plane—yet. I was satisfied with my progress although I hadn't any money to show for it and was oblivious to a fermenting, ruinous situation with my obligations in the States. I felt, nonetheless, that I was progressing and would never need to return to Milan, which proved to be false. After all, I had a big show, a great contract, and a lot of hope. I flew off to Hamburg stoned, with subconscious, deep-seated resentments that I would soon associate with the whole of Germany.

FuckedUp InTheFatherland 06

Aurora's apartment was located in a fashionable residential area of Hamburg. The building was stately, and the apartments were large. Aurora had a one-bedroom. The living room had elegant, floor-to-ceiling windows draped in wispy, white curtains and overlooked a public green area. Unfortunately, an odious smell permeated the room, due to the digging of a mysterious, deep hole just outside her window. Aurora continually lit candles and burned incense to rid the apartment of the evil that we imagined lurked there.

A white futon, where I slept, lay against one wall in the living room. It was here where everyone sat most of the time. Everything else—ashtrays, candles, incense containers, stereo system—was on the floor. It was an apartment that one could easily get around in by crawling, which is exactly what we did, and what we were normally capable of. When not with her current, horrific boy-toy friend, named Craig, Aurora slept in her bedroom on a never-made bed. Prior to my visit, she only used the sparsely furnished bedroom as dumping grounds for her clothes and partially unpacked suitcases—preferring to pass out on the living room floor futon.

My experience with Aurora would only add to the combination of other harmful elements that would work together to drive me to the edge of a nervous breakdown. In my continual downslide into addiction, I easily projected the unresolved issues with my deceased father onto the city, its people, and its environs. Hamburg was the ancestral home of my father's family—my grandfather Adolph was born there, and my family name, Reincke, came from a medieval Hamburgean fairy tale of a fox. Growing up, I hated everything about the male posturing of my father and the men in his family and their subordination of the women. It offended me that men were restricted

50

in how they could behave (overtly masculine only), what they could talk about (sports and limited other subjects), their interests (intellectual pursuits were looked down upon), and how they could interact with one another (drink and compete).

Equally tiresome were the limited responsibilities of women: cooking, cleaning, tending after the children, and discussing women-things in the living room, while the men drank themselves into fools in the kitchen—activities that my mother disdained. Mom couldn't hide the fact that she was different from others in this family, with an aristocratic heritage, intelligence, and beauty. I was always attracted to these qualities in her, and we were always very close. I would later learn that his brother ridiculed my father for this and for not otherwise inciting me to fight, roughhouse, or act in a manner that denoted traditional masculinity. In reality their father's Hamburgean twin brother was gay and in a long-term relationship with another man (my mother didn't tell me this until well past a decade after this trip). My parents were so misinformed—products of their time—about why a boy turned out to be gay that they actively pursued methods to influence my sexuality by, for instance, not allowing my father to exhibit any outward physical signs of affection.

My old roommates, Lothar and Rudy, and their girlfriends, Zoë and Romy, were also in Hamburg, which gave me a feeling of security in an otherwise unfamiliar and psychologically traumatizing environment. Less comfortable were the entourage of male model friends that Aurora introduced me to that first day. One was her hairdresser and drug dealer, and another five physically perfect über-men were her party buddies, disco friends, and a lover. The possibly straight hairdresser was rude, coy and arrogant. The equally possibly straight boy models were unfriendly, boastful, and aggressively egotistical. Except for the one moment when any of these boys shook my hand, they wanted nothing else whatsoever to do with me. None of them asked anything, barely made eye contact, nor made one single attempt at conversation. The feeling of invisibility evoked a sadness I felt from years of denying my true, exuberant self.

Aurora's drug of choice in Hamburg was ecstasy. I had no former experience with this drug, but, as a pothead and trusting in my friend, I eagerly participated in trying something new. Ecstasy was quite unlike the pot, hash, or alcohol highs I was so familiar with. It made me feel I intensely loved everything and then dropped me into the void, as its strength waxed and waned like a rollercoaster traveling around blind curves in the fog. With night fallen, and me high on a drug I had no experience with, Aurora did what she had always done—left me to go out with her bad-energy friends. Unable to float off to other partiers as I had in the Giusti, I spent the next several hours alone incensing the apartment and feeling relatively good while trying to scratch in my journal. I managed only words, "ETABS, She is Beautiful, Enya, Candles, Light, Warmth, cool leaves, Subtle orange, greens, powder blue, and friendship." Aurora woke me up when she returned home the next morning at 7:30 a.m. We smoked four joints, and then I passed out again until 7:30 p.m., which ended my initiation into life with Aurora.

The Hugo Boss show would be in ten days on August 6. In the meantime, as in Paris and Milan, I realized I had to go out and sell myself again. My father used the term "hustling," which I despised because it had such an unpleasant and demeaning connotation to it. What it meant to Dad, who had to pay rent since he was ten from his newspaper route (for real), was that you had to "work hard to feed your face." But I understood that this was necessary. I needed an agency in Hamburg and had to get work. Underlying all of the other issues, and one that wouldn't easily go away, was my slip into financial destitution, which would become a new experience for me. Monday would be an important day for me to represent myself well to the agencies.

It would have been preferable for me to set appointments with the German agencies through my Milan agency. This didn't happen. I ended up calling all of the top agencies—Model Team, Louise, and Pro-Mod—on my own. At least my mention of my representation by

Ugly, my having been booked for the Hugo Boss show, and acquiring a contract in Tokyo, allowed me to visit the agencies at my own scheduled time instead of the mass castings normally held for want-to-be models.

I carefully considered how to dress. My black linen shirt, open a few buttons at the top, with my black jeans and boots, didn't seem to be right for humid July Germany. But my cream-colored, permanently wrinkled pants and the preppy collared shirt that I used to wear as a Hewlett-Packard employee did not feel right either. By the time I had thrown something together, my body had moved into full withdrawal from the consistent partying I had been doing for weeks. I was hot, uncomfortable, and befuddled by the summertime humidity so much like that of Michigan. With a bad haircut, puffy face, wrinkled outfit, and haunting paranoia over appearing effeminate to everyone including the pedestrians and passersby of Hamburg, I hopped into my first cab.

First, I went to Liza at Louise who looked at my pictures and told me to come back later after I had seen the other agencies. I'd heard *this* before. I then saw Gitte at Model Team. I was too short—a quarter inch below six feet. I had failed the absolute cutoff of the German height restriction. They based this on the logic that male models needed to be taller than their female counterparts, who, in Germany, were leggy and tall. I was beginning to feel depressed.

Inge and Sabine at Pro-Mod said that I needed more tear sheets to make it in Hamburg. How ridiculous I thought. In Paris, maybe you need them, but not in Hamburg. Who was she kidding? I finally went back to Louise to discover that since the others didn't want me, neither did she. Going to a lesser agency just didn't seem fitting as I really didn't know any and, even though German markets were working in August, work there was slow too. "Fuck Hamburg," I wrote in my journal that day.

Journal, July 27: *For the first time in months I don't feel like a model. I feel like Robert. It's pissing rain outside again. Sleeping weather, but I'm going* *shopping, cleaning and feeling like a house-husband to my beautiful and glamorous model wife who is off working, having her pictures taken for the world to see. I'm happy and resolved in my heart, in my faith, and in my desire to see the world one last time so to speak. Northern Germany is not my place either. It is cold and somehow bunkered in. There is hatred against foreigners and this city is ruled by Fear. Perhaps the summer warmer climate of Southern Germany will be more my cup of tea - and more editorial*

Ever the optimist, I hunkered into the role of househusband to Aurora, who, though still getting work, bitterly complained about her new case of "red-eye." I cleaned the apartment and used a little map she made for me to get some errands done. I needed money and a train ticket; I had to laser copy my book and mail it to Japan; I needed to contact the comp-card developer in Milan, send the cards they had made to Japan, and put the cost on my account—all of it a very tricky business. I also needed to fax Tokyo and ask them where in Cologne I was to pick up my airplane ticket.

As the week progressed, the pleasant feelings I had my first night began to fade. The hole outside took on a more sinister tone. Sitting on the dirty futon, I began to imagine specters swirling up from the bowels of the earth—lost souls of time immemorial ever haunted by Germany's wars and atrocities. Added to this I pondered why nothing was happening sexually between Aurora and me despite the fact that I felt nothing sexual for her. Lying frustrated, stoned, and silent next to Aurora's exhausted, inebriated carcass feeling pointlessly rejected by her and shunned by my agencies, I wrote the following in my journal:

Journal July 28: *I'm in the trap again. Stoned from morning to night. My emotions, feelings and thoughts are held ransom in the brick tomb I've created for them. I care for maybe even love Aurora…and now, now is when I have been blessed with the opportunity of being alone with her. She even told me last night that she was lonely. I felt unable to rescue her only…saying that I was lonely too. Do what then – attack her physically? Lie on her, move my hands on her body – just reach over and kiss her? She's too frightened. She used her kissing karma* *and assertiveness on Craig and not me.*

Why am I always in this trap since grade school. Watching from afar the girl I really dig being involved with some other guy who always seems to come in the picture to distract her right at the most critical times or me just fading out – normally on the excuse of drug induced lethargy at other critical times. She met up with Craig while I lay asleep in bed after chain smoking 4 joints with her… Everything about Aurora excites and even entertains me. Would she lead to my eventual self destruction because I would feel as if I was impotent in my ability to entertain her, be there for all her needs, and keep her mind focused on me?

…the only thing I'm getting off on Aurora is that I'm a good and trusted friend. She likes boys and I like girls but if we love each other we can trust that will keep all of the rest away. I'm so confused, tired and cold. Pray. I'm almost afraid that I have too much need and will be unable to give as she needs. That I'll be found out for the lonely and inexperienced maybe even shallow guy I was.

The problem is…I don't have any money. Modeling is the most difficult thing to get into right now. It's not the 80's. And I spent the 80's spending my dads money on a fuck ass MBA…Aurora called. Curled up in her bed. Cold. Cold and gray. Feel like crying. Aurora called. She's working. I'm 20 again. MSU. Christmas passes. [a girl…a boy] God Help. She'll call at lunch again.

I've taken 3 dumps. I'm so cold. I'm so afraid. I feel out of control. I haven't the answer. Where is Harold and Maude. Why can't I devise a plan. Why do I have no comfort. Why is there only bleakness? Why can't I see the light or feel the heat of the sun without the suns presence. Where have I gone wrong? Where have I turned off? Is there a way back on? The identical, bored, pained green eyes of the 14 year old boy across from me on the train were significant. They were a warning and they stared something very powerful within me – even a sexual stirring but not directed at him just within. I was warm and physically aroused but just internally. I was barely focused – barely alone numb.

The following day things went farther downhill. I faxed Tokyo again, only to discover I needed to charge the ticket on my credit card and trust them to pay me back. If this wasn't unpleasant enough, I called San Diego and talked to the girl who was supposed to be making payments on my car—she wasn't. My demoralization continued in my doomed effort to woo Aurora. I bought wine and chocolates for her. That evening, I noted "we hung out all night sleeping, listening to music, and drinking bottles of wine...I threw-up and thought of dying."

Humiliated by my sexual defeat, rejected by the Hamburg job market, and failed in proving my manhood to myself and the ghosts of my ancestors, I fled to the train station the very next day. There I bought one ticket to Wiesbaden where I would visit my distant relative, Tante Gerdi, and a second from Wiesbaden to Cologne, where I would perform in the Hugo Boss show. After I had anchored my escape route, I returned to Aurora's apartment to prepare for an evening that would truly be the culmination of my German angst.

Our goal was to go to the Havana Club where we were supposedly to meet Lothar, Zoë, Britney (a 16-year-old friend of Zoë from the Giusti), Rudy, and Romy. I was somewhat looking forward to seeing everybody, although I had begun to take Aurora's view that they were boring—I had been so involved in her world I forgot that I had anybody who cared about me. The adventure was reminiscent of the time I took my first drink—a time crucial to every alcoholic and one which most remember. Then too I was torn between my group of simple but sincere friends (who I had become bored with) and another, more exciting group who invited me to join them but with whom I didn't feel accepted.

Once Aurora returned from her job, we went over to her hairdresser and ecstasy dealer. There Aurora spent a lot of her hard-earned money on pills for me, her boys, and herself. We both swallowed a tab immediately. It hit hard and fast as we rode in a cab towards the decadent, soon-to-be dreaded *Reeperbahn* party/sex district. I already had a bad impression of it because the *Reeperbahn* was where Aurora spent so much of her time away from me.

Once at the club, we popped another ecstasy, and Aurora transformed herself into the beguiling vixen of the evening. She then moved into the groove and onto the dance floor amidst her admiring boys and other nameless partygoers. I watched her swaying and gyrating with the rolling, swooshing feeling of the ecstasy tablets that were kicking into our bodies, souls, and minds. Music pumped a driving techno-beat. The dance floor swirled in eerie flashing colors. The red, blue, and turquoise reflected off mirrors that also caught the shadowed images of strangers cloaked in clouds of cigarette smoke.

Before I knew it, Aurora was out of sight. Feeling awkward standing alone, I bumbled past throngs of strangers as I tried to find her. For a moment, I bopped around, feeling isolated, self-consciously dancing amidst the foreign celebrants. I began to panic. People crushed in every space. Where was she? I began searching again—seeking Aurora and myself. I needed to save her…to save me…to save us. I needed to seek, to find, to reconnect. The music blasted and the colors seemed more pronounced. Everything moved up and down. I rushed…thrashed…bruised…through the crowd. I looked for the exit. I thought it must be the other direction. People seemed to be staring at me—I had dressed in my sexy, sleek model best. But where was the door? How would I get out? There was one of Aurora's boys. Maybe he…can…tell…me…where…the…door…where Aurora was? I felt like I said something and he said something…outside.

The air outside hit me with cool mist as I stumbled and perspired to the curb where Aurora was smoking a hash joint. She asked if I was all right. She said that I didn't look good and that I should sit down. She asked if I wanted a hit, and I took one. Then she left me with the rest of the joint and proceeded to go back in with two of the boys also sitting there. I started to feel a bit better, and then reverted to feeling like a loser. Why couldn't I go in? Shouldn't I go follow her? Shouldn't I go show them that I was having fun dancing with myself? Shouldn't I be able to compete? Was it hopeless for me to learn their language? This couldn't be. After all, I did have one good thing going for me: I had a great tolerance level and proved myself time and time again with my ability to drink and smoke with the best of them.

Crazed but conscious enough to remember this, I went back in.

Nothing had changed. The lights, fog, insanity, illusions and delusions, and paranoia…all were still there. The ecstasy was in its element there, and it hit me with its full force. Lost and afraid again, I knew not how to go home. Just where was home? Whose home was I going to? Where were the soft, clean sheets of my childhood bed in Michigan? Where did my Biffy Bear ever go? Where was my grandmother's *streusel küchen* while we watched a rerun of *The Honeymooners* and I got to stay up past eleven? Where was the comfort of surfing that perfectly breaking, warm summer wave? Lost, I felt completely hopeless. And then, as if in a dream, I saw Lothar, Zoë, and little Californian Britney come towards me with the cool chill of the evening air on their clothes. It wasn't long before they grabbed me and took me to the door. Zoë didn't like these places, and Lothar wasn't comfortable there either. They walked me out into the refreshing night and then to their car. I sat in the backseat and told them of my fears. Lothar said I was tripping. He said I could just be still and relax. Everything was all right. They were taking me away. We were going to the cottage in the countryside that Lothar's family owned…the cottage…the countryside. There would be a flower garden and clean sheets. It would be quiet. I could find my sanity there. They were taking me to safety. The soft misty breeze blew into the open, backseat window of my friend's family's car. We were going to the country home where he had grown up. I'd find lace doilies on the tabletops. I was going home—to his home. By the time I snuggled beneath the down comforter it was 6 a.m.

The Hugo Boss Show 07

What a relief it was to wake up in the peace and quiet of the countryside—at the reasonable hour of one p.m. Indeed, the country house had all the charm that one might imagine a quaint small-town home to have. The living room was flush with doilies on armrests, tabletops, and beneath candy bowls. The kitchen, decorated in wood and crystal, had wooden tables, chairs, cabinets and pantries with crystal vases, glasses, bowls and candleholders.

We all had a delightful, full breakfast, during which everyone, including Britney and Zoë, smoked cigarettes. I started to feel more down to earth, albeit a dirty earth. But grunge was in and my morning-after ensemble of gray t-shirt, black jeans, and black leather belt with silver buckle looked fine as Lothar draped long beads over my neck. We showered, and everyone agreed to go with me to Aurora's to retrieve a clean change of clothes and the rest of my possessions. I would be spending the rest of my time in Hamburg at Lothar's apartment in the city. My near-mental breakdown was sign enough that it was time to leave Aurora and her boys—my San Diego therapist was right; women like Aurora had the capacity to destroy me. Aurora wasn't there, however, and she would never learn the rationale behind why I would thereafter shut her out emotionally.

After helping me to pick up my stuff, Lothar took me on a tour of my father's family's ancestral home. The sky was gray, with a heavy humidity that made me feel somber. It soon began to drizzle. We drove back to the cottage where I phoned my mom—a weekend ritual I performed religiously. We then wandered the fields where Lothar played as a child. We climbed trees, took photos, and released our adult anxieties, which wasn't too hard for Britney or Zoë since they were still children. Adding to our little foursome's happy mood was the interesting predicament that Britney had a crush on me, which she had maintained since the Giusti. But she was 16 after all. This allowed me to not question my lack of sexual interest in her. I treated her like the sweet little girl she was.

We then went to a small village called Kirkbert. A charming restaurant stood on top of the hill. The day was so gray that haze shrouded the views from the path leading to the restaurant, which normally provided majestic views of the surrounding countryside. We continued anyhow. The inside of the restaurant was similar to Lothar's family home and full of carved wood cabinets, doilies, and china. It provided the perfect backdrop for the warm apple tarts and coffee we enjoyed. Feeling at heart unworthy of such domestic bliss, I wanted a drink. The setting reminded me too much of the clean German home that my mother had tried so hard to create for me. Indeed it was truly evocative of my grandmother's house where I had spent many days of my childhood actively engaging in behavior that could be defined as "the best little boy in the world." My frustrated and stifled inner-child was dying to get out. I only had patience for engaging in cute, familiar activities for a limited time. I, nonetheless, maintained the composure I once had easily maintained, knowing that the time would soon come when I could drink or drug myself out of consciousness.

After finishing our meal, as the drizzle turned to rain, we returned to the city and Lothar's apartment where we watched movies—an activity that easily entertained our teenage girlfriends, who relished the slumber party nature of the experience. Watching movies was difficult for me because I lacked the capacity to focus, follow story lines, or comprehend what was going on for very long. Consequently, I disdained the activity altogether. Fortunate for me, as day turned to evening, Lothar, too, was anxious to get out. We went to his drug-dealer's house, purchased some hash, and danced with the girls at a place called the Garage. I never considered that going out dancing at a club the day after I recovered from a drug-induced near-nervous breakdown was a bad choice. Fortunately, we didn't stay long. Upon our return, watching more movies until after 6:30 a.m. was sustainable because we now had weed and I was already drunk.

By Monday morning, after spending Sunday hiking, mushroom picking, and watching yet more videos—including personal recordings of Lothar's Tokyo modeling experience—our little ritual of pleasant breakfasts had turned into a nightmare, and I "freaked out." Keeping up the facade of domestic tranquility with the routines we had established had become more than I could handle. Rain for many Hamburg summer days, just like in Michigan, had made me claustrophobic and angry. So I hopped a cab back to Aurora's and promptly got lost en route. Once I finally made it there, I noticed that the apartment was even more uncared for than it had been. I found my U2 tape and umbrella—my protection from psychological and physical storms—and hung out. I realized the Hugo Boss show, the main event of my summer, would be in four days (the next Friday). I knew I was a mess and floundering from one bad situation to the next. Life *was* safer at Lothar's, so, two to three cabs later and lost on the streets of Hamburg, I eventually returned.

The next morning I said bye to everyone, which included stopping by Aurora's and once again getting lost on the way to the train station. It was to my great relief that I would soon be out of Hamburg (which I held responsible for taunting and confusing me), and on to Niedernhausen where I would visit my elderly, peaceful distant aunt. Once at the train station I met "Sunny," who was from San Diego. I took this as a good omen that I was heading in the right direction.

The problem with visiting Tante Gerdi in Niedernhausen was this: it was with her that I had my first alcoholic slip after my first attempted recovery two years earlier. I had been three months newly sober when I made the poor decision to leave the country. Gerdi had no understanding of what an alcoholic was. I was young, 27 at the time, and had a good job. How was it not possible for me to control myself by having a simple glass of champagne, she had asked. I eventually agreed with her, which led to progressive increases in alcohol intake for the rest of that trip. The difference then was that I came back to the United States and got back into recovery. This time, I was out of recovery completely and with no intention of ever returning. Nonetheless, I behaved like a good boy, drinking moderately as I spent the next three days with her.

What had always followed my jaunts into acceptability was the growing schism between the proper, refined and subdued me, and the frustrated man who sought healing and acceptance for who he really was. Long walks with Gerdi in the misty German forest behind her apartment left me feeling stifled, bored, and itching to run. By the time I departed my aunt's quaint town, I was ready to party hard. The nadir of my drinking experience in Germany was soon to come.

That afternoon (Thursday, August 5) I arrived in Cologne to throngs of male models checking into the SAS Royal Hotel. Overwhelmed with so many beautiful guys, I felt uncomfortable as I often did among large groups of men—fantasizing that they had the self-knowledge and confidence that I lacked, and judged me for it. Instead of waiting in line to check in I marched directly to the bar. Oddly enough, there were no other models drinking—perhaps they wanted to appear to be on good behavior at first.

After gaining my prerequisite numbing buzz, I checked-in and then went to my first scheduled activity—a 4:30 fitting. There I learned that I would be part of the "Hugo" group of young, upcoming models that were to be representing a new line of clothing marketed to younger professionals interested in trendy fashions. A second group, "Boss," would be composed of older, established stars. A third group which I couldn't remember and didn't write down (the Baldassarini line) were composed of models who would wear the new sophisticated brand of Hugo Boss clothing meant for expensive, distinguished tastes. I was pleased to be in the young category, even though the casual clothes—based on un-Hugo-Boss-like baggy sweatshirts, overalls, and a new Arabian look—didn't suit me.

After my fitting I returned to my room, where I met my preassigned roommate, Ricardo, from Brazil. Ricardo was slender, young, and relatively short. He had the newly emerging multi-ethnic look that was making its appearance on the runway. This outweighed his lack of physical stature. He also had a classicism that Italian casting agents and designers preferred. Both elements were appropriate for the conservative yet exotic appeal that the Boss people were trying to project. I felt that my own Slavic-Germanic looks, mixed with my classical awareness, were perfect for the circumstances as well.

Ricardo's outward beauty mirrored itself on the inside, for he had a calm serenity. Spending the evening with him alone in our room getting high and listening to whale sounds would have been beautiful, if only I could have been more present. Unfortunately, I knowingly worried about my state of mind. I had looked forward to not having any hash on me, but it yet again surrounded me. I knew my old acquaintance, paranoia, would surely find me as well. The last thing I wanted at such an important event.

The next morning the grandeur began. An event in which 70 international, male models would need to be rehearsed, made-up, dressed, and changed as many as four times in collections that represented a lavish attempt for Hugo Boss to regain preeminence that it had only four years earlier before the high-fashion clothing market began its downward spiral (it succeeded). It would be an exquisite festival beyond compare. Nearly 3,000 would be in attendance. The entire compound called "The Fair" was made up to represent a festival of Greek gods. Hundreds of feet of gossamer fabric billowed around gargantuan male and female statues and framed passageways leading to an enormous tent. The runway, shaped like a T, had an enormous metal openwork structure at one end in which scores of male models would climb and pose for the finale.

At 7:30 a.m., we were shuttled to a separate rehearsal hall that did not contain the elaborate catwalk. We would not be able to rehearse maneuvering the metal apparatus, which the two groups of models representing the new lines (Hugo and Baldassarini) would have to climb. I felt silly, self-conscious, and foolish. Walking down the runway, in my homophobic-mindset, still seemed something that sissies did. The other models took this dead seriously.

After rehearsal we were given time to relax. Ricardo turned the whale music on again before meditation, which he suggested I also try. He then got high and asked me if I wanted some. Despite the fear of being paranoid and sabotaging my performance, I immediately said yes. What would it hurt I thought? This would be the time when I would finally implement the strategy I had devised when I first started smoking pot. My convoluted rationale for ten years to that point was the following: since I was normally uncomfortable around people, if I could learn to eliminate feelings of judgment while making myself even more self-conscious by smoking pot, then I would be less nervous than I was when not smoking.

As usual, my experiment did not work. So I drank as an excuse for my need to compensate for heightened anxiety. At 5 p.m. we were bused to the event where we would then have three hours before the show started to have our hair and makeup done. I vaguely recall a bottle of schnapps between my legs and a joint being passed. Slightly swaying, we arrived. Walking through diaphanous curtains and between what appeared to be several 20-foot-tall, white Michelangelo *David* statues, to the back changing area was breathtaking. The problem now was time. It seemed I had a lot of it. The little make-up and slight trim job needed for me wouldn't take long. So I mulled around at first with some of the other guys from my group—mostly longhaired, young, hip British boys.

A group of what appeared to be Hugo Boss executives sat around some of the long plastic tables and chairs set up near a side corridor. Considering this area also for models, I felt uninhibited in nibbling from the paltry snacks in plastic plates on the tables. I also noticed many bottles of champagne and plenty of plastic, fluted glasses. Looking around and seeing that no one seemed to mind, I filled a glass and offered myself a toast. It felt odd standing around as the model I had become and recalling once being one of those more refined, mature-looking business people. Disregarding the slightly dirty feeling I felt, I then wondered why so few, if any, other models weren't there drinking with me. I filled up another and perhaps a third quickie—champagne always seemed like water.

Events blurred more after that. I recall the professionalism of a mirrored wall of stylists and make-up artists. Rumors spread of the size and importance of the audience made up of a dizzying array of photographers and journalists, agents and editors, buyers and retailers, celebrities and wealthy patrons from the world over. I snuck out, took a peek, and gave my video recorder to an Italian man who said he was with the show and would film it for me. In order to relieve my quickening anxiety, I darted back one last time to the tables of champagne. Once there, I felt lonely and letdown. Why wasn't anyone else here too? Weren't models supposed to be reckless partiers?

Events continued to become hyper-dramatized after I made it back to wardrobe. My group, wearing the baggy, red sweatshirts and overalls, were the first to go out. It didn't matter if I had drunk every bottle of champagne on the table and smoked pot until charcoal came out of my mouth—I was still all too present. Fortunately, as rehearsed, we all lined up and walked as a team. Lights sent out a UFO-type glow from every angle. Music pulsed and probed. The sidelines were dark, but I knew that in the darkness loomed thousands of super-judgmental people.

I knew I was supposed to keep a straight face, but had no idea how. What I wanted to avoid most, especially when we all turned at the end of the runway, was to keep from smirking. I knew, from the first set of professional tests I ever had, that I had the capacity to create a smarmy look—slightly upturned lips and googly eyes that didn't look like the sexy, confident guy I thought I was supposed to portray. If that happened here I surely would die.

As I continued to walk, every cell in my body reverberated with insecurity. I screamed at myself that I was less than, that I was not equal to any of the people sitting there, taking the pictures, dressing me, designing the clothes that went on my pitiful rack, or that walked side-by-side with me. Feeling fully a masquerader, my mind screamed, "You thought you fooled them but you're the fool because you're an IDIOT, you're a MORON, and you DO NOT FIT IN HERE!" Through these self-berating thoughts, I conscientiously practiced looking aloof and unmoved, pleasant-not-angry, sultry-not-shitty, with a clenched jaw yet full lips and my lower eyelids slightly upward so as not to reveal the horrendous whites below the pupils.

Several rows of photographers stood on platforms at the end of the runway. This would be the worst and last torture. I wobbled towards the end, so self-conscious that it was impossible to recall anything I had learned about posing for the camera. Thoughts progressed to "It's only this moment…this one infinitesimal moment of life in the entire world and universe and all of time…PLEASE GOD JUST NOT THAT SMIRK!!!"

I reached the end. Cameras flashed with so much light that I could have been having a near-death experience. Jesus didn't seem to be there though. Looking directly into the lights and out to the millions upon millions of people I imagined the photos would manifest themselves to, I made the Mona Lisa smirk with wide-open, big, blue/green eyes just as I had feared. I felt an immediate sense of horror. I believed my pose was so awkward that it would have made the rotted-out portrait of Dorian Gray look appealing. The trauma of my internalized self-judgment combined with the sobering affects of the moment, incapacitated me to the point of perhaps not making the turn and arduous walk back.

I remember only a blur of men's bodies changing in-between walks, helped by as many hands as could fit into cramped quarters. Feeling I had already failed, I don't remember the subsequent two changes. The last was in the first outfit again—but some guys went shirtless. It required our group to climb up the metal monkey bars and to sit. Oddly enough I did so without incident.

Walking on the stage below us in their tuxedos and after-dinner wear was the group Boss models. Feet dangling above, I had contradictory feelings. Why wasn't I one of those models, I thought jealously. After all, I was gorgeous, intelligent, sophisticated, and had an MBA. Then my logic reversed itself again, "I must really be a loser since I'm not one," I resolved. As applause faded, I climbed down with the rest and we all walked onto the stage as a single group .

The post-show change was as frenzied as the rest, since so many models where throwing their clothes off at the same time. Male models argued with assistants and designers about keeping their wardrobe. No one could keep their outfits. But I overheard that a couple guys had gotten away with walking out in theirs, which sounded like a good idea to me.

I changed my shoes but kept my final Hugo Boss outfit on, grabbed my backpack and headed for the exit. As I began to walk, I noticed another of my group doing the same, complete with his overalls and baggy red sweatshirt. As we made it to the coagulated bunches nearest the exit, we stopped. But as the crowd of eager-to-leave models, hairdressers and stylists, moved towards the security guard at the final squeeze-out, I barged ahead. Then, as soon as I could, I found a bathroom and switched back into my own clothes—happy to look like a civilian once again. Once in the common area, I retrieved my camcorder, worried that the man who recorded the show would have something mean to say about my performance—he didn't.

Models, audience members, and many others who chose to, were shuttled to the after-party held in a large hall. It had decorations similar to "The Fair," mainly life-sized Romanesque male statues draped in white cloth. A central stage was in the main room, with adjoining rooms and bars in each corner. Not wanting to drag my stolen Hugo Boss clothes or video camera around, I rolled the camera in the clothes and handed it to the security guard at the front entrance for safekeeping. She (I believe the guard was a woman) placed the folded heap on the center table directly between the two front entrance doors—not a very good idea.

Masses of distinguished guests crowded in. German Hoffbrauhaus girls, wearing dirndles that pushed their breasts up, came in from the city to hand out drinks and cigarettes. Another group of similarly clothed drag queens attended as well. I immediately grabbed a couple of packs of cigarettes from a Bavarian wench and two drinks from another. Despite my self-perceived failure at the show, I kept company with a couple of acquaintances from my group. Becoming quickly bored with them, I ran into one of the British boys who told me he was getting high in the back and invited me to come. The side alley was dark and had a lone car parked in it. It felt strange being back there with him and his friends, and I felt oddly concerned with the legality of what we were doing. Soon the others left, leaving him and me alone with the joint. Interestingly, too, I wasn't hungry for the pot. But I smoked a little, staying close to the boy in our back-alley secrecy.

Before I knew it, we shared a kiss. I moved forward so that he was pushed to the hood of the car—possibly my first assertive gesture towards a man. Suddenly, for no apparent reason, he decided to leave. Alone again, I definitively re-entered the sultry party, feeling afraid, vulnerable and exposed—as if everyone was aware of what I had just been doing with the boy. The crowd seemed larger and unfriendly again. I drank vigorously.

By the end of the evening that was mostly a hallucinogenic blur, the floors appeared caked with gunk, and the curtains seemed less white and tattered. My drunkenness and fear made a nightmare out of the memory of the event. I later recorded how wrong it was to get so pissed and dance with transvestites on the podium—"Who am I, a Christian or a wild crazy man?" I wrote. When it was finally time for me to leave, finding the door was very difficult. When I did locate it, of course my camcorder and the Hugo clothes were no longer there. Frantically, I located a security guard.

The man, in what I came to understand as a typical European

means of getting rid of drunk Americans, pretended not to understand much English. He then seemed to say that he had been there all along and never saw the items. But he was a *he* and the first security guard was a woman—I couldn't have been that mistaken. When I had entered, I was more or less sober compared to the state I was in by then. Angrily I asked others, to no avail. I had lost my camcorder and the final tape that I so diligently recorded. At least I would never have to see the replay of the runway show that I felt I had performed so poorly in.

The first acknowledgement of my existence the following late afternoon was the good-spirited goodbye of my roommate Ricardo. He gave me his number and the gift of a leather bracelet he had made, a Hugo Boss bottle of cologne, and the sincere request that I visit him in Brazil or New York. I apparently freaked out and then later felt ashamed of my behavior towards him. After Ricardo left I became extremely disoriented, lost, frightened, and confused. I had never in my life felt like this before. There was no way I was going to be able to checkout of that hotel and go. Where to? I had no place to go until Tokyo, which wouldn't be until the 18th and it was then only the 7th. How could I pack my bags and schlep onto public transportation? I barely knew where I was, let alone how to get to another destination. I hardly knew *who* was occupying my painful body and mind.

I called downstairs and asked if the Boss Company would pay for another night. "No," they told me—I'd have to put it on my credit card. I knew at that point I did not have the capacity to get up, shower, pack and make decisions. I COULD NOT function in the world. I gave the receptionist my credit card number, not caring how much it would cost, and rolled back under the sheets feeling alone, afraid, and empty. Dead inside, I truly felt that my very essence, my spirit, my soul, had up and left.

A few hours later, I couldn't deny physical hunger. I needed food, but couldn't bear the thought of the cost of room service. I forced myself to get up, shower, and walk outside. It was early evening and the church bells rang. Still exhausted by my alcohol-poisoned body,

I felt as if all the suffering that town had experienced throughout the centuries had coalesced in me. In misery, I felt I had contact with the spirit world. It became important to reconnect with my lost soul. In a subtle way, through the kiss of the boy, I was.

I found the magnificent Cologne Cathedral, one of the most beautiful historical landmarks in Europe. I went inside, sat, and prayed. I don't know how long I stayed, but when I left I experienced a flush of fresh air. I started to feel more human—just one of so many normal people now that all the other models and fashion people had left. I knew that I'd at least be able to figure out where to go tomorrow. I "ate some sausage" (says my Franklin Planner) and "decided to become a minister."

The following day, I bought a business-class plane ticket to Munich, where I had an invitation to stay with my Tante Gerdi's niece, and wrote in my journal:

…God is leading me in the right direction. I only don't understand my own passionate screams to him of God damn it or feelings of wanting to just throw myself in front of a car and kill myself because I'm so lost and cold and tired and ~~worried or unsure~~ *and miserable. Just remember Faith, Trust, Don't Worry.*

LeGranBleu&
ChocolatePudding 08

I arrived in Munich to the orderly, well-kept home of my distant relatives—a beautiful, stately woman, her husband, and their young child. Interestingly, Brittany was there in Munich, too, and had invited me that first night to a house party. It was the last time I saw her. Unfortunately, I remember nothing of it. The next day, feeling tired and sick, I got horribly lost, which seemed to be my theme in Germany, on my way to the Munich branch of Louise Models. They promptly informed me, "right look, wrong time."

My sweet relatives kindly allowed me the space and comfort I needed by giving me their child's bedroom to sleep in. Two days of rest and moderate social drinking with the family and their neighbor left me feeling antsy for more. This quickly became intolerable. By Wednesday I wandered out of the house and into the Englischer Gardens, Munich's main park, where I found the aggrandized hippy, gypsy feel I so longed for. Although I never really knew or experienced the true grit of hippidom, the core of my understanding of what it meant to be a hippy was expressed by the newly monied boomers that romanticized the reality. Once in the park, high on hash and in my desired ethereal fog, I conversed with an elderly man who, with an all-knowing countenance told me, "you are the star of your own movie and can do whatever you want." Finally, I had the authoritarian Germanic approval that I was free to live my life as I wanted. I chronicled the rest of my day's activities in my journal:

Journal Wednesday August 11: *What a great day it was, and it wouldn't have been such a great day if I stayed secluded and depressed in my room. It was the forcing myself to get out and deal with all sorts of people that has helped to rebuild my confidence and my health. This scary masked ogre of a person who wouldn't leave me alone in the park. The girls in all black that I got high with* *and these strange friends, the dude from Encinitas and the other psyched out young boy doing acid until he fries out his brain even more than it seemed to be. The Festival—the modern day hippie carnival and Woodstock—that is the Englischer Gartens of Munich. The hoity toitie snobbery of the Schwabing restaurants and the waiter who would not help me and didn't speak either English or German to me. He, the waiter, snubbed me and I'm sure would have taken more money from me if he could. And then also crying to Whoopi Goldberg and watching "Made in America" in German with Germans. The boy who at first seemed hostile to me at the phone booth, but then after talking to him, not only gave me some hash but also let me use the phone first to call Britney. I've learnt that above all other aspects of my personality, the first most obvious is that I am an American. Funny because earlier in the day and week I was most identified as an Englisher. I don't fully understand the people and their ways but I can get by and I am immensely more proud of myself and confident. I am Robert the American.*

The following day I returned to the park for more of life's lessons and contemplations. There, while sitting on a hill in the twilight, I spotted a black man on another hill across from me. He welcomed me over, shared his smoke, and explained to me that he was the "Black King" and the mound we were sitting on he called "Little Africa." I shared some of my hash with him too, and he proceeded to tell me the story of "Le Gran Bleu."

Le Gran Blue—the name of a real or imaginary dwelling—began when a black man, after having slaved for many years of his life for others, decided to sell all of his worldly possessions and move to the Gold Coast of Somalia, where he could buy a little piece of land. Once there, he bought his dreamed-of property and promptly built a beautiful home. The house looked out over a blue ocean and warm seas. A white, sandy beach lay before the sprawling veranda. Gentle breezes blew across the hammock-filled porch. One day, sitting on his veranda amidst all this tranquility, beauty, and serenity, he realized that others should share it. And so he decided to open it to people with peace loving thoughts and a common goal of the unity of all mankind. It was there that all who came could rest and stay as long as they liked.

The Englischer Garden Rastafarian told me that I seemed to be one of those people. If I liked, and ever found myself in Somalia, I could go to Le Gran Bleu. We continued to smoke shared joints from each other's supplies and as the sun began to set, he invited me to come back to Little Africa.

On my way out of the park, I bought a necklace of green African stone and wood made in Somalia and then stopped at a pizza parlor close to my relatives' home, named Queens' Pizza. There they served me large mugs of strong, German beer as my bohemian garden afternoon transformed into a far more perky night. I met a "hippie brother" named Oli who invited me to his house to play cards with a gang of friends and his lady, named Emma. Oli called himself the White Bavarian King. Not having been a cocaine user, I missed the metaphor of "white" to mean "cocaine," which was plentiful that night. Earlier that day, the Black King had warned against using hard drugs, so I abstained for the time being.

Night turned to a stay on his couch, which turned to the morning of Friday the 13th and a horrific hangover. But Oli—who I learned was a mail carrier and whose friendship would thereby karmically ensure the safe passage of any mail I sent while in the city—gave me "power through his hands," I wrote. He and his woman also taught me how to roll a joint with a cardboard filter and hold it without shaking (a true king would never smoke a joint with shaky hands, I was told). We returned to Queens' Pizza, where I played a game of billiards against a cute, young German guy and won, which I took to represent "victory over all my masculine fears." Later that night, back at the White King's, I again won, this time at poker, which further renewed my sense of self-confidence. After sleeping once again for a few hours on his couch, I finally returned to my relatives home to collect the worldly possessions I carted with me like the vagabond I had become. After showering my partying off, I again stopped by Queens' for a free beer for the road, took the U-Bahn to the train station, and transferred to a rapid ICE train back to Hamburg. Two days after having met a Black

King, a White King, and eating at a Queens', and feeling acceptance from the land of my father's because of it, I proceeded to write the following journal:

Journal Saturday, August 14: *Power from the kings. Power from the Rastafarian man and Le Gran Blue in Somalia. Power to live, to think, to be free…to dream to hope to envision! Power of acceptance in a brotherhood of mankind. Power of acceptance and concern for the world.*

Power from the White Bavarian King. To wander, to explore and test and create. Power to truly feel and to give and to receive comfort, protection and acceptance without judgment, friendship without judgment. Honesty and being straight with oneself and people.

From the Black King came my strength to abstain and refuse the offerings or temptations of hard drugs. From the White King power to deny the fear of myself. To just stop. To be and not fear. From the white boy at Pizzeria power to gamble and win! From God above all the gifts that these kind traveling companions have offered, the food, the rest, the communion of goodness that is left.

Rows of sunflower fields pass by. Sun flickering as it darts between tunnels. Train briskly charging beyond. Behind is München – Recovery, Camaraderie, Confidence at making it Alone, Growth, Wise men who help.

Once I arrived in Hamburg, Lothar picked me up at the station and drove me to Aurora's to extricate the remainder of my clothes before taking me to his dealer's to party until five in the morning. The next day, Sunday, August 15, was as bleak as I had remembered Hamburg to be for me. I woke up at one p.m., watched MTV while Lothar studied, and wrote in my planner, "cranky and bored, no one really talks or relates." Stuck at Lothar's in a drizzling rain, I longed for the freedom I was constantly striving for, yet which remained fleeting. Amidst my growing sense of wanderlust, I remembered Paradise—the bar in Amsterdam that the White Bavarian King had told me about. An immediate urgency to find this utopian place took control. I told Lothar that I was going to go. He obligingly took me to the train station. This would be the last time I remember seeing Lothar although according to my Franklin, I would see him again in Milan and Paris.

Through the windows of the train, I saw sunflowers and felt embraced by the freedom and comfort travel gave me. As the train passed into Holland, it became legal to smoke pot in some cabins. Gleefully I joined in the merriment with all the rapture of the free-flowing sixties that I had heard so much about but was born too late to experience. I met a group of two guys and a girl from Amsterdam, Austria, and Greece, who invited me to hang out and share a room with them. I refused, instead agreeing to hotel with a group composed of two girls and one guy from London, whose ratio of two girls versus two guys seemed more acceptable.

Once arrived in Amsterdam, I immediately scurried over to Paradise—a bar with menus of pot food, pot drinks, pot to smoke, and pot-smoking devices ranging from paper to bong to pipe. Thrilled, I ordered a bag of "sensi" weed and took a big hit. The pot didn't do much. Soon I realized how alone I was in an empty bar smoking, eating, and drinking pot in the middle of the afternoon. I left to search for the other bar that I had been referred to—Soul Kitchen—but never found it. I had yearned for a feeling of disconnected freedom, but had found only loneliness. As a result, as I continued to smoke my way across town, I bought 18 postcards to send to every person whose address I had back in the states to finally tell some of what had happened to me, and others of the joy that I was supposedly experiencing in my new life.

Many more bars, lonely highs, and two days later, I woke up knowing that I would be leaving for Tokyo the following day and had to get to Munich in order to catch my plane. I called my agency in Tokyo that morning before I checked out of the hotel, then went immediately to the train station to get my ticket. I bought some marijuana cake (called "space cake") to take on the plane with me, drank some marijuana tea, smoked the last of my skunkweed, and caught a train out. I looked for the sunflower fields, but this time there were none other than in a little painting I had purchased.

The first train stopped in the city of Osnabrück, where

I transferred to another train headed directly to Hamburg. There I would have to wait for six hours before transferring again to the train to München. The new train no longer allowed pot smoking as the Dutch trains had—a fact that I did not despair over, for, by then, all the pot in Amsterdam could no longer get me high. The crowd on the Hamburg-bound train was much more conservative. A middle-aged woman sat next to her daughter across the aisle from me. Next to her daughter was a friendly looking, handsome, well-dressed man. I paid little attention to the thirty-something man other than perhaps a furtive glance. Knowing German, I began a decent conversation with the mother and daughter.

As the train came to a stop, the man, who introduced himself as Vova, having overheard that I had a long time to kill, asked if I had seen the sights of Hamburg. I immediately answered "no" despite the fact that I had seen parts of the city—through the ends of joints and under the sparkle of disco balls—with Aurora and Lothar. Vova said he would be happy to show me around even though it was quite late. I felt a tug of nervous anxiety. As we left the train, I asked the middle-aged woman what she thought about taking the handsome dark-haired man up on his offer. She shrugged her shoulders and either said or indicated that it was okay and up to me. Having gained her approval, I excitedly agreed.

Vova's first suggestion was that we walk to his penthouse apartment where I could leave my bags. I followed him up a hill above the train station. As we walked, he asked me if all the jostling and bumping in the train made me a little excited. He shared that it did for him. Feeling excited by his comments, I agreed that the jostling on the train must have made me horny too.

Having sex with a guy wasn't new to me. When I was 25, one year after my first sexual experience with a woman, and between girlfriends, I had sex with a young man my age who had belonged to the same fraternity as I, and who I met while visiting another fraternity brother in Chicago. Gil did everything to me that night, including fuck me. I loved it all—nothing felt more natural. When Gil left the next morning for work as a banker, I lay on his bed and watched him get dressed while I felt completely safe and good. I then snuck out of his room, only to find his roommate, another fraternity brother, asleep on the couch. I said nothing and for years blamed the experience on being drunk and high. I later used it, incorrectly, as part of my unsuccessful rationale as to why I was an alcoholic and needed to get sober. For the five years prior to this trip, I dated women—many who tried in vain to gently guide me on how to hold them, feel them, or fuck them. They were of differing ages, nationalities, races and religions, and I proudly recorded all of their names, which I later drew from on this trip, as a measure of my possible bisexuality.

Several months before I ran away to Europe (my subconscious plot to come out), I had another experience with a man. Ian was one of the friends that I started drinking with again after my full slip back into active alcoholism. He adored me in every way (primarily, because he respected me for being sober), and although I never found him attractive or interesting, I kept him as a friend because he wanted to be. One day he confided that he felt a lot of shame because his sexy, blond, "straight" surfer roommate had asked for and received blowjobs from him. I had been a surfer and secretly—even to myself—found surfer guys to be extremely hot. Not long after that and too drunk to drive, Ian spent the night in my condo. I recalled lying awake in my waterbed visualizing the surfer; how it would feel to be him; and how he felt being blown.

My vision came true, as all of a sudden I saw Ian standing by the door. He said nothing, and neither did I. He slipped in to bed and started to give me the blowjob I had secretly longed for. It felt wonderful. Later, drunkenly floundering on top of him, he told me I could fuck him. I didn't, afraid that I would hurt him. The next morning, when he asked me how I was doing, I lied and told him, "No big deal." But it was. I was terrified with myself and never had sex with him again. More distressing was that I slowly found reasons not to hang out with him, completely abandoning his friendship by the time I ran away to Europe.

In Hamburg, Vova and I didn't even make it back to his apartment before we started fooling around. We arrived at the top of the hill near a set of park benches beneath some trees. It was dark, and no one else was there. We sat next to one another, and before I knew it, he had unzipped his pants and begun stroking himself. Inspired, I did the same. Neither of us touched each other, although I, as always, wanted him to make the first move. What if he really didn't want to touch me? What if he really wasn't interested? I felt it would be more comfortable to lie down. Perhaps he'd touch me then. So I did, right there in the grass. He followed, and eventually grabbed my dick. I grabbed his. Immediately he decided that we should continue our walk to his apartment post haste.

In the apartment he showed me to the bed, where I enjoyed lying down again. He took off my shirt and pants and proceeded to give me a blowjob. He then disrobed except for pair of clean white socks—exposing his beautiful, firm body. Having had so little experience and being so self-absorbed and overwhelmed by exhilarating feelings, I passively lay there, missing opportunities to enjoy and reciprocate in kind to him. The last of these episodes, he got up from crouching above me, and went into the kitchen. He told me to wait and re-emerged with some chocolate pudding. I had no idea what he was doing, although I think he asked me if I liked pudding, and I responded that I did. He covered my chest, nipples, and penis with the dessert and slowly, carefully licked it off. I came but selfishly have no memory if he did or not.

Time evaporated, and I realized, still covered with leftovers of chocolate pudding, it was getting closer to my departure time for Munich. He offered to take me out to eat. I was oddly calm, but didn't mind the thought of a drink. He also offered a shower, but I preferred staying chocolaty. We went to a pleasant outdoor café near the station where I had a big beer and some fries. He gave me his number and told me that he was an anchorman for a local news station. He wanted to see me again if I ever came to Hamburg. I took his number, aware that Hamburg would be off my radar for quite a long time and grateful not to have to see him again.

I caught my train and arrived in Munich at 9:00 a.m., still covered in chocolate. I then walked by the embassy and picked up my papers to go to Tokyo. Afterward I stopped by my relatives to finally wash the chocolate sexcapade off my skin and say one last *Auf Wiedersehen*. On my way out of their quaint German suburb, I stopped one last time at Queens' Pizza. My heterosexual friends were there getting drunk in the middle of the Wednesday afternoon. I felt weird. In the short time since I had last seen them, I had crossed the line from trying my damndest to act, feel and be just like a regular German guy, to having been eaten by one—to my great-denied delight.

I made my way to the airport where I caught my flight north to Frankfurt/Main Airport, and then transferred to the 6 p.m. flight to Tokyo. Onboard I opened my carefully wrapped "space cake," which reeked of pot, and ate a chunk. I saved the rest for later. It would be a long flight.

I reveled in the naughtiness of being able to get high while flying over Russia en route to Japan. Technically, I had gotten stoned in Germany—my father's family's Fatherland—and then over Russia— my mother's family's Motherland. The extent of insanity in Tokyo would make it No-Man's-Land, I'd soon discover.

Surreality 09

My long flight arrived at last in Tokyo at 3:00 p.m. on Thursday, August 19, a hot, humid day. I took a limo, as instructed, directly to my Agency, Team. Akasaka, Tokyo, the area in which the agency was located, was in a high-end part of town, but typical of much of the architecture used to rebuild Tokyo after WWII, it contained a multitude of generic, international-style buildings. The ground floors of these office buildings harbored expensive restaurants and posh grocery stores, which sold such items as individually wrapped fruit at exorbitant prices.

Team was exclusively located on an uppermost floor of one of these 1970's, box-like buildings. There I met my head booker, Michiko, who introduced me to the rest of her staff of women. Everyone smiled daintily and slightly bowed their heads. This formality, unusual from what I had experienced in other modeling agencies, and other subtle differences in eye contact and body language added to my sense that things would be different here. I would learn that Michiko and her staff were special compared to what I eventually saw in other Japanese office workers. Though she looked demure in appearance, working as a powerful agent in the international realm of fashion modeling necessitated a strong constitution, iron will, confident determination, and long, 12-hour days. I would later hear a model-rumor that the Japanese mafia—the Yakuza—controlled the Tokyo fashion and modeling world. This, I was told, granted models a form of immunity, which resulted in the outrageous behavior and use of drugs that otherwise was so contrary to the rigid social mores I witnessed there.

After filling out paperwork and allowing the Agency to take my passport and make copies of my driver's license, I sat in a plastic chair by the door and waited for the driver to come pick me up. Unlike

Italian agencies, where other models hung out and hobnobbed to gain favoritism, none did so here. A driver named Noboru, a amiable man about my age, eventually arrived after escorting other male models (men were separated from the women) to their last castings. Our team consisted of seven young European and American men who had lived in Tokyo for various lengths of time—some of whom were married or had girlfriends. Interestingly, there were no Japanese or other Asian models in our group. I was told the Japanese preferred European-looking models and therefore used those in more than 50% of their ads (although this percentage was dropping as Asian models became more desired). Noboru's job was to drive us around town to castings so that we would not get lost in the confusing array of sometimes-Japanese-language-only metro signs. Soon I would learn that our air-conditioned home-away-from-home had an awesome sound system that allowed us to rock-out to The Black Crows, Morrisey, Jamiroquai, Depeche Mode, Lenny Kravitz, Social Distortion, and U2.

Noboru took me straight down the boulevard to the Rappongi District, where I was housed. Rappongi, I was told, meant "six trees," though no one I spoke with had any idea where the six trees were or if there ever were six trees of any mystical quality there. From what I was told, the area had developed as a tawdry, reckless bar area that served the American military base, which had ensconced itself nearby after WWII. It maintained some of these elements as it grew to include other, more fanciful and sophisticated bars, discos, and nightclubs, making it the international center of Japanese party life. Exorbitantly priced, high-density apartments and neon billboards also lined the expansive boulevard, which throbbed with the beat of the nightlife I would very soon experience.

Further down this same boulevard from my agency and past where I would soon live, stood a replica of the Eiffel Tower, which was slightly taller than the original. Unlike the original, it was painted orange and surrounded by the aforementioned, generic buildings. It took my roommate and me several weeks to build up the curiosity to visit this monstrosity. Even the Japanese rarely acknowledged or visited the site. Yet it was one of the very few cultural sites that we took the time or had the inclination to bother with.

When I arrived, the weather was tropically hot but quickly became wonderfully mild and sunny except, that is, for the occasional typhoon. During typhoons the normal sounds of the city were disrupted. At other times the rancor of loud and boisterous nationalist protests against foreign (and particularly U.S.) intervention could be heard. These included blaring announcements from bullhorns on roving vans and marchers tremulously waving flags and shouting indecipherable slogans in their native tongue. As my time progressed, the sheer force, noise, and disturbance of these groups made me feel uncomfortable as an obvious, although privileged, outsider.

The apartment was in another poorly constructed, thinly insulated, 1960's building. I would immediately learn that it would cost my roommate and I $2,000 a month each, which compared to the $700 that I had been paying (and needed to still pay) for a coastal condominium in Southern California was disproportionally expensive. This cost, along with the added costs of my flight, my weekly expenses, all office expenses such as faxing, photocopying, and mail, new composite cards, and the cost of the Team book to hold my photos, would be deducted from what I thought was the $10,000 promised me on my contract. If I was fortunate, money that I earned above my contract would be payable to me minus the agency fee of 20%. If I had read the contract, I would have known that the agency fee was actually 45% and that my contract was actually for $13,000. But none of this mattered because the implication of financial guarantee made me feel sheltered—just as I felt as a child.

The interior of the apartment appeared more dismal to me than its squat four-story exterior. Rice-paper-thin walls separated its two bedrooms, one bathroom, and a kitchen. Uniquely Japanese features included a kitchen sink that reached only to my pelvis—even lower than the sink in Milan, thereby creating constant embarrassing water stains on my crotch—and equally low or small countertops and appliances. Luckily, the toilet was standard European-style and not the hole-in-the-floor variety that in some older places would require one to squat.

My roommate, Tom, had the larger of the two bedrooms, which contained a standard sized window with a miniscule view in the upper right hand corner. My room had a window that opened directly out to a noisy, cement and steel stairwell. I, at first, kept this open to protect myself from the stifling mid-August heat or the dirty air of the unclean window air conditioner. My twin bed had pale, worn bed sheets and a skimpy coverlet, which were functional given the early heat, but grew less so as the temperature dropped. The carpet was motley 70's, dirty brown mini-shag.

Most telling of all, however, was a large, pink 10¥ phone that sat on the kitchen table. In order to make phone calls (and only local calls were allowed) one needed to feed 10¥—less than a penny each—into a slot on the top of the phone. My new roommate had learned from prior tenants, who had learned it the same way, that if you shook the phone very hard, the 10¥ that you fed into it would come out the bottom. One could then reuse them after the phone call. It was important to maintain some 10¥ in the phone because Noboru, who I'm sure knew what was going on, was occasionally sent to clean them out.

Tom, my new roommate who was originally from Atlanta, had a well-built body that he used to make a lot of money selling underwear and swimsuits for catalogs in the U.S. and Tokyo. He was short for a model, which was typical in Tokyo, where average people were shorter than in Europe or the States, and therefore the models who represented a supposed ideal were also not so tall. Tom had a wife and two kids in Atlanta whom he called every Sunday; yet he had loud, ecstasy-laden or coked-up sex with Japanese girls quite often. This bothered me, not only because it sometimes woke me up, but also because I greatly disapproved of infidelity. I discovered that if I partied

83

later than he, which came naturally anyhow, I wouldn't have to worry. Sometimes Freddy, a fellow Team model and friend of Tom's, came over to fuck a girlfriend of Tom's girl-for-the-night. This was worse because I could clearly hear through the paper walls that separated me from the kitchen. I imagined him going at it on our kitchen table, the low counter, or on the few stained chairs we sat on in this common area. This greatly added to my living-space nightmare since I enjoyed residing in a clean and organized environment.

My first day in Tokyo ended with an introduction to one of the places I would spend a lot of time—the Java Jive lounge. Java Jive was a restaurant/bar where models received free coupons for dinners and free watered-down, hellish, well drinks, or a punch concoction made with fruit nectar and grain alcohol. The dinners—a total of six—were Japanese versions of American standards and more nourishing than what would be our staple Mini-Mart food. Other bars and discos that catered to models and charged a hefty fee for civilians included Spirals, Vieties, Buzz, the Gas Club, and the Panic Club. I would spend many nights at these places, yet have no memory of the fabulous conversations or incredible experiences that would have warranted my spending so many hours of life there. Too exhausted to take in much that first night, I settled for a couple of screwdrivers before crashing on my decrepit, little bed in my expensive hovel.

The next day my roommate escorted me on the 25-minute walk past the bars, the noodle and sushi restaurants, and finally the pricey markets, restaurants, and fashionable business district, to the agency. Once there, as in Milan, I immediately caused a stir in my relationship with the head booker. Saving face—a concept dear to the hearts of the Japanese—was not something I knew much about. Bothered by my accoutrements, I thought it was important to let her know in front of my roommate and all the other bookers that there was a hole in one wall and a crack in the window, so that she could see to having them repaired. She courteously acknowledged my request—a response that meant absolutely nothing.

After this unusual check-in (which Michiko must have orchestrated to make sure that I wasn't a fuck-up), Tom and I climbed onboard the van with Noboru and went to our first castings. Castings generally started a little later in Tokyo and numbered between one and six on any given day. The agency opened at ten in the morning and closed at eight or nine at night (it closed at 6 p.m. in Milan). Jobs could start as early as six in the morning, however, and required use of the subway or a prearranged pick-up by the client. Michiko's first-day strategy was similar to Hobbes' in that after my check-in, she sent me to two of her top clients, a catalog mainstay of the agency, *CNC Family Club*, and a top editorial magazine, *Men's Club*, to gain feedback. I eventually worked for the lesser paid, but more prestigious magazine.

Having experienced the elitism associated with European editorial work I fancied myself a part of, I snobbishly looked down on catalog and commercial (printed advertisement) work. Unfortunately, as was true the world around, these jobs paid more despite providing less interesting photos. They were also the primary work in Tokyo, and competition for catalogs had been increasing—one no longer automatically booked good jobs because they were fortunate enough to have a top agency as in the past. Much as in Germany, the best strategy—and one that was just becoming known—was to go to Tokyo, establish good reputations with clients, and make as much money as one could. A model would then have enough money to survive going back to markets that were more editorial to get the tear sheets or tests needed for better jobs in bigger markets—this strategy also worked between Germany and Italy and was what Aurora had successfully employed. I also didn't understand, at first, that any money I made in excess of the contract amount was all mine after the agency fees and taxes were paid. Not comprehending that I needed to "hustle" every job I could to pay back that contract, I considered, as I had in Milan, that the editorial jobs would be a better long-term strategy.

After our first two castings, Noboru picked up the next model. Sean was a "dude from Kentucky" who had a sexy, lean, muscular body and was the youngest of all the models—22. Most of his jobs were for swimsuits or underwear like my roommate. His modeling composite card also positioned him as a cavalier Southern Gentleman, thereby increasing the range of commercial work that he was mostly suited for. He was short like Tom and most of the other male models, which made me one of the tallest. Secretly, he turned me on.

The rest of the afternoon, which conveniently happened to be a Friday, entailed a body casting for Sean and Tom, dropping Sean off, picking up another model for yet another group casting, and returning to the agency where we picked up our weekly allowance. That day and every Friday to come, I received 20,000 Yen or approximately $200, which was supposed to cover all of my living expenses outside of rent. This money did not go far in a city in which an average restaurant bill could easily surpass this amount, resulting in my most elaborate meals being conveyor-belt sushi, and the need to supplement my income by taking cash advances from my credit card (with no chance of any additional earnings until my contract ended, I was told). Bills in San Diego would have to take care of themselves. Fortunately, my condo was being rented. Unfortunately Shannell had not made any effort to make a Jeep payment—a fact I would learn more of as my time in Tokyo continued.

That Sunday my new modeling friends taught me my first Tokyo financial trick. Tokyo's large central park, where, as in parks in Europe, one could buy drugs if they were in a bind and their connection was out, also catered to another black market—illegal phone cards. In order to make long-distance calls one needed to utilize a public phone booth that took a special Tokyo phone card. A group of men dressed in traditional Arabian garb worked the park selling ten cards for the cost of one. They did so by repairing the holes that a mechanism in the phone produced as time had elapsed on the phone card. By consistently purchasing these cards, I was easily able to affordably contact my mother and grandmother for our usual Sunday calls and the bank in the States, my condo homeowners' association woman (fees I never paid), the real estate agency (that only once was ever able to rent my condo), and Hobbes at Ugly to see if I was in demand back in Italy—not to worry.

Drinks and drugs were the least expensive items of all since access to them was easy. In every major city and most all the clubs, models entered without having to wait in line and drank free or cheaply. Additionally, Tokyo came conveniently complete with inexpensive beer, caffeine, and tobacco vending machines that sold all of these items until late at night. One was directly across from my apartment and served late night, early morning, or mid-afternoon, affordable beers on demand. Because, at first, I had no pot or hash to moderate my buzz, I drank a large amount of cheap and easy-to-get booze.

Quickly, however, I found a solution to the missing ingredient in my inebriation cocktail—hallucinogens. One of my Team models, Bram, introduced me to absinthe. Absinthe—a form of alcoholic hallucinogen—was illegal in most of Europe and the United States, but had once been quite popular with artists, aristocrats, and bohemians with whom I so desperately identified. They would drink it in early 20th Century La Belle Époque cafés, the historical period and location I often dreamed that I belonged in. Bram was married, like the other Team models, and Dutch. Short, with a thin, elegant look, defined cheekbones, noble nose, and a sultry lower lip, he was both gorgeous and dangerous. Bram was glad to find camaraderie sharing the liquor so closely associated with his great, fellow compatriot, Van Gogh. The painter used it before cutting his ear off, so says a long-standing rumor. Bram told me all about absinthe history and the stultifying effects his first experience had on him, which included seeing material items appear as floating waves and the walls of an elevator appear translucent. Three shots would be unspeakable, he said. Transfixed by his story, I rationalized that being a model, much like a 1970's rock star, meant experimenting with drugs to open the doors of perception and aid in my art. Indeed, the professional photos of the time had been morphing into images of drug-induced otherworldliness. Perhaps, I concluded, this was one of the reasons why I had found myself in Tokyo—the outer edge of the planet.

My memory of my first introduction to this new drink was insignificant, although, according to my journal, "I came to grips with cigarette smoking and Christ" because of it. The following day, after a callback for the prestigious *Men's Fashion Magazine*, I took it upon myself to introduce absinthe to Tom, Sean, and a third model, Alexander. (Alexander always bitterly complained that he did so poorly in France not because he was too short, but because he was French and no country liked models of their own nationality, which, except for the U.S., was mostly true). No one was particularly enthralled, preferring boring beer instead, which began my disillusionment with their lack of sophistication. Growing weary of their simple ways, I would shortly thereafter seek comrades that were more entertaining. Annoyed at not having the fun I had hoped for, and the realization that despite getting a job, I still wouldn't see any more money soon, I decided to write in my journal as follows:

Journal August 25: *So here am I. Tokyo. So what have I? A job next Thursday and Friday. Other than that, an agency that is trying to push me and friends that say "lets see what happens." Don't give up. I'm in debt big time. I had four shots of Absinthe - a codeine, opium based drink and I'm not even drunk any longer. People like me but so fucking what. The client's who pay aren't really biting yet. I need them to bite. I owe, I owe, I owe and don't even have an audition until 2:30 tomorrow afternoon. I can just sleep forever. But it's hard to sleep here in this city that stays up all night. Where traffic at 2:30 Tuesday morning is like rush hour any other place in the world. Where there are always other models ready and willing to stay up just as early as I could ever imagine. I drink and smoke but have come to peace with smoking. It's OK. God does not condemn me for it. I live in a dump that costs $2,000 per month. I'm worried though I try not to be. My brain is soggy but I'm learning.*

As was typical, my youthful ability to rebound had me jogging and doing sit-ups the next day. I got a haircut, called the Visa Gold helpline to find out how much money I had left, bought the book

The Road Less Traveled, and stopped by the agency where I hung-out presumably to gain favoritism, even though this was ridiculous to do in Tokyo. At day's end, which concluded my one-week anniversary there, I wrote in my Franklin that I finally began to feel comfortable and then went to bed early. That weekend young, sexy Sean and I spent a beautiful sunny day together, which ended with him getting me high on pot for my first time in Tokyo and introducing me to a drug connection—a local named Thane. By Monday morning I smoked dope before an important second go-see with a respected Tokyo photographer. Tuesday I not only got high with Bram, but also agreed to have some absinthe before my biggest day of castings yet—with all seven Team models—where I finally experienced the effects of the liquid nightmare. Oddly, I remember it all.

Instead of riding in the backseat of the van, I floated. Feeling as if I was operating in an illusion, or different reality, I was strangely aware that my visual and auditory nerves came from some physical body, but not sure whose. Noboru suddenly opened the side door of the bubble that was our rocking-out, air-conditioned van to let us out for a casting. The shaded windows had slid away to reveal the horrifyingly bright sun hideously glaring off the concrete buildings. The muggy thick air attacked me. I sat immediately immobilized as my mind sprung into its insatiable self-conscious fear that everyone was hyper-aware of me and my inability to function in the material world. Everyone got out but me. Noboru waved me to come. I refused. He eventually conceded, but told me that he couldn't leave the air conditioning on, and he proceeded to escort the other models to the client.

I gained some sense of equilibrium as the inside temperature equaled and then surpassed the outside sweltering heat. Realizing that Noboru was the eyes and ears of the agency, I determined to get out and try. I shielded myself from the sun, got out of the van and crossed the street to the strange house that served as the casting place. Once inside, I noticed the stairs were concrete slabs on steel that jutted out of the wall without connection to one another. The last of the guys was already springing down them. I took my shoes off as was customary at some castings, and carefully made my way up to where Noboru was waiting. Once at the top I stood against a wall. There I was once again blinded by a flash of light. This time as a Polaroid was taken.

Polaroids were routine at all Tokyo castings, which differentiated Tokyo from other countries in which Polaroid prints were only occasionally used on jobs. They allowed the client to have instant record of how the model looked in person, and the photographer to see how the model, lighting, and set-up might appear at a job. In Tokyo, they were nearly always horrible looking, and models loved to either tease each other about them or compete for the rare good one.

I waited a moment while the horrific image began to appear on the photo I was handed and then was gently nudged into a room with a plastic chair in the middle and a panel of scary-looking men in business suits. I sat on that chair petrified, sweating profusely, and quickly averting my glances as they looked between my beautiful pictures, the horror that was the Polaroid, and the pupil-dilated, bedraggled, lump of a model who was sitting before them.

My memory of the remainder of the day is sketchy, although some of its details remain in my planner. It was that afternoon when I ate an uncustomary (because it was expensive) Big Mac and fries and ran into my Milanese friend and roommate Trent. I believe we made plans to run into each other in the swirl of bar hopping that occurred throughout that night. I have no idea if we did, and never ran into him or saw him again. Terrifyingly hung over, I woke up early the next morning at 7:30 a.m. to clean the apartment and pray. I was too frightened to call the agency, so I called Bram instead to find out what the castings were. The following hot, humid night required that I keep my dirty air conditioner on all night. I slept poorly and woke up early a second day in a row—this time at 5:30—to go to my first Tokyo job.

My first job, two weeks into what was supposed to be a ten-week stay, paid the agency 82,500 Yen or $825 (minus the agency fee of 45%) towards the $13,000 I owed. The shoot was a two-hour drive from Tokyo in a coastal resort town. It was billed to be for a sporting catalog but, fortunately for me, had nothing do with sports. The client picked me up in front of my apartment in their van. Once it arrived, I met a sweet-mannered, beautiful Belgian boy named Luuk who sat cordially in the backseat and would become my best friend. Luuk was a classical model with an angular face, blond, slightly curly hair, blue eyes, and a thin but tall 6'2" stature. In one of our increasingly conversant, intimate nights, he shared with me that he had always felt different from his peers because he was dyslexic—a fact that gave me empathy for him since I, too, had always felt different and had my own handicap (ear problems). Despite this, he read a lot, but didn't go far in school, which made him feel further ostracized and sometimes insecure— another fact I loved about him. He had a fiancé back home who loved him greatly. But he wasn't sure he loved her as much. Interestingly, Luuk also knew and liked Lothar whom he came to know when they had been in Tokyo together. Together, we affectionately coined our mutual friend's litany of antics as "Lotharisms."

The shoot that day consisted of two shots with Luuk and I, one alone, and one with me and some girls. As usual, the Polaroids I kept were atrocious. The make-up artist had caked my face with foundation to cover my already pasty complexion. She then added rouge to my cheeks and lips to bring out the redness. The boxlike coats I modeled were more like a costume, making me look like a Mao impersonator—not a very good likeness for a Japanese photo shoot. Additionally awkward was that I was requested to smile, which I had little practice in—most of my work had been more somber—and gave me further cause for discomfort. Luuk moved with grace, knowing how to move and pose consistently in front of the speedy lens—a trait I told myself shouldn't be too hard to learn.

Afterwards, he invited me to his penthouse apartment. It was luxurious, well-furnished, stocked with videos, cleaned regularly by a maid, and had a commanding view of the entire city—ours was cleaned once in awhile by Noboru. His luxury made me jealous. Ever since entering the labor force with my first job in Chicago, I couldn't help but notice the discrepancy between the material wealth of some people and the new sense of deprivation I was experiencing. It seemed to me that this differential existed regardless of (what I perceived as) my excruciatingly difficult effort and their lack of industrious activity. Though I liked Luke, I didn't think he was all that more handsome a model than I, and therefore didn't deserve such a markedly different living space. (Which, if I would have had the objective capacity to analyze it, was contrary to my deeper belief system of unjustified born privilege, since in modeling one's looks equated to one's ability to make money; this was just as much a born privilege as being born into a wealthy and generous family). Luuk and I spent the rest of our first evening together talking and watching *Monty Python* and *The Last of the Mohicans* before I retired to my hovel. The next day, I dropped a 10¥ piece, which sat next to the giant, pink phone, and called Michiko. I then gave her a two-week notice on my apartment. The threat was idle, as I had no idea where I might move or how I would pay for it and did nothing to find out. Michiko would soon have a justifiable response. In the meantime, she took my shocking news with the reserved, good taste I knew to be her hallmark.

Tripping Models Over Tokyo 10

The weather threatened with its typical September typhoons as I spent what would have been Labor Day in the U.S. trying to put my life in order. I called Milan to find that the cards I had ordered and paid for were hopelessly lost—Michiko had already made replacements, which she charged to my account. I called Hobbes to discuss my stolen camera and see whether he had heard anything from the Boss people, to no avail. I called the condominium homeowners association to see if my contact, the president, had received any money for the possessions in my condo she had mostly giving away—no money there and lots of lost goods. I then called my mom to find out about my Visa, which I knew I might have to use later in the week, and went to the gym, which had closed. Given no castings that day, I decided to smoke some hash marijuana and go to a bar with Sean. After several drinks, we played a game of Foosball. I proudly disclosed for a full page of my planner that I nearly won.

I always took an interest in male athletes at school, and the best of them turned out to be acquaintances of mine. From my earliest memories I rarely played sports; when I did, I purposefully lost, thinking that a win would mean more to others than me. I feared that if I engaged in competitive activities, I would lose myself in wanting to win so badly that I would go to any extreme to do so. In the end, I had the unresolved guilt that if I had participated in sports more when I was a boy my father would have loved me more. But, in truth, I had at one time played baseball with a winning team, and it didn't make all that much difference to him—Dad was just incapable of expressing love.

The small and seemingly meaningless activity of playing a drunken game of Foosball with Sean in a late-night Tokyo bar brought

93

up an array of complex emotions surrounding my relationship with Dad and other men in the Michigan of my youth. Despite my childhood disdain for family members that drank too much, I was partying with more zeal and reckless abandon than I had witnessed in any of them. In Tokyo, Sean's and my partying the rest of that night continued into the rest of the week and beyond. I drank absinthe on Tuesday and Wednesday with Bram despite having to go to work—luckily the van that was supposed to pick me up never showed since the job had been cancelled due to an oncoming typhoon (I got paid a cancellation fee for not working, which seemed much better to me). By then, my food was as bad as my addictions warranted, consisting of donuts, sushi rolls, and noodle soup from Styrofoam containers purchased at the Mini-Mart. By the end of the week the extra money I was spending on hash, a useless gym fee, food, and cigarettes ended when the ATM machine no longer produced anymore cash, which was the first time that had happened. It horrified me.

As my financial crisis worsened, I responded by clinging deeper to the most melodramatic religious tenets and finding more excuses to drink and drug harder. I wrote in my journal that "…he who is higher on earth will be lowest in the kingdom of heaven; spread the word—the end is coming around the corner; good people are losing their minds and souls in this industry; and I am nothing but God's pawn." Despite my first job for *Max* being in print in international markets, I was too numb to care. It was not worthy of any emotional response in my journal, Franklin, or memory. What was more important was noting that I smoked weed with my roommate's trick while he called his wife that day. By the following Friday, after Michiko brought our advance money to the apartment—because we all three had job "tickets" for work within the next three days, and she may have wanted to get a personal look at the place I considered so atrocious—I hungrily used half of it to feed my addiction to hash. As usual, despite knowing I was not benefiting myself by this behavior, I also could not embrace a solution, as disclosed in my journal that day:

94

Journal Friday, September 10: *My lungs are heavy with the stain of days inhaling not only the humid, polluted air, but also the cancerous smoke of packs of cigarettes weekly since Milan. My head is not in any normal frame of reference nor has it been almost daily since Milan. Drugs, alcohol, tobacco and some good (long) sleep have created quite a salad in my brain and I'm beginning to seriously FUCK UP again. I'm fucking up because I'm not myself but becoming that partier who all the guys think is too cool but who really is a wretched loser who never quite seems to succeed. And what's worse is I'm nervous, anxious, and displeased with myself on a continual basis. I know this modeling thing as anything else will* <u>*NOT*</u> *click until I become straight with myself again. But I'm already afraid of the withdrawal.*

Nearly a month into my contract I went to my second job. The theme of this photo shoot was sophisticated yachting attire, which they shot on sailboats at an exclusive marina. It came complete with the pancake makeup that had become customary to cover my mottled complexion. Once again, I had no idea how to wear the jackets I wore without them looking like ridiculous plastic boxes. The other male model on this job, like Luuk, was highly adept at this catalog work. He was also extremely handsome, solid, and manly in every way (I noted in my journal that he was a "real" man) and would soon become my second heartthrob.

Besides a great body, Scott had a wonderful, playful spirit that reminded me of the phantom love of my life, Petey. He was also represented by Team, but got around on his own, had his own apartment (since he had been in Tokyo for quite some time), and went to a different nightclub from my gang. He preferred a bar called the Lexington Queen, which was a dark lounge that didn't offer models free drinks and attracted a more sophisticated clientele than the rowdy clubs I was more familiar with. He also had his own unique cadre of friends represented by a different agency (Cinq de Un). As time progressed and I got to know him a little better, I happily discovered that he was one of the few men I ever knew that was mature enough to talk about issues outside of work, sports, or girls—instead he talked about life, philosophy, being happy, and having a good attitude.

The day after this long, lackluster job that I did not appreciate and wanted to end, Michiko called and told me to come into the office. There I was told that I would be terminated in four days—I'd need to leave the day after the job I was to shoot that Friday, which was for *Men's Review*, the client I had first seen when I came to Tokyo. Ironically, the two-week notice I had given earlier would have also been effective that same day (which was exactly halfway through my contract). Had I read my original agreement, I would have known that the agency had the responsibility to terminate model contracts after 30 days if the model did not obtain at least ten jobs, which I obviously hadn't.

I pleaded once again for my survival, making sure to put on my best-boy appearance that had gotten me out of trouble my entire life. The result was that Michiko agreed to discuss my status in the agency later. My first instinct to recover from this excruciating calamity was to party, which I did—I drank free margaritas at Buzz, danced at Java Jive, and left the Panic Club at 5:30 a.m. Yet I knew even more strongly than before that I needed to change. So I worked on changing my thinking. I wrote in my journal to appreciate everything; to get over my superiority complex; and to stop picking on myself for crimes I had not committed to God. Furthermore, I decided to appreciate my roommate more. After all, I noted, he showed up for his underwear modeling work on time and sober, and did a consistently good job. I realized and noted that Michiko worked hard every day in her office until very late at night—my complaining and demanding had gotten me nowhere. I concluded by deciding and writing that I would try my hardest to respect everyone and, above all, not to argue.

By Thursday morning, I was granted a second chance—I could stay out my contract for the next 30 days. But my new attitudes faltered. The night before my big editorial job, I took Sean to the Lexington Queen. I had once before met Scott and his clique there, and vibed that the bar, like the boys, had a different quality that I took as more genteel—a quality I found attractive though I felt was at odds with the likes of real men. We drank voluminous quantities of bourbon that night and smoked even more hash later. Since I judged Sean to be a member of my straight group of friends (although I didn't know this to be how I intuitively differentiated groups of men), I felt weirdly outed by bringing him to the Queen, which catered to gay men, although I didn't consciously know this. Drunk, conflicted, and confused I later vented my feelings in my journal. Unfortunately I never identified anything having to do with my true mix of emotions and only scribbled that Michiko was to blame for her failure to get me more work and begged my deceased father to help me find a way.

Horrifically hung-over the next morning, my torture increased by having to go to early castings before my job. Luckily, it was Noboru's birthday and he may have been too preoccupied to bother with telling Michiko about my condition. We all sang him "Happy Birthday" as we rode around in the van. When I signed the inside of his birthday card, the guy next to me pointed out that the picture on the front was of a naked man. It was the first time I realized Noboru was gay—a fact that seemed odd to me since he seemed like such a normal guy.

My misery remained as I walked to my photo shoot. I knew that even my youthful body wasn't magically popping back to the fresh look I needed to pull this off. My hands trembled, I felt edgy and sweaty, and I knew I looked pasty and pale. As I continued, I noticed vending machines for caffeine gum, cigarettes, and beer. Needing immediate resuscitation, I bought all three. They didn't help.

Esquire owned this magazine, I understood, and the standards were exemplary. The photographer, assistants, and stylists, were professional and the wardrobe exquisite. Like the Max job, there was only one "look," in which I wore a beautiful, long black trench coat over a double-breasted navy blue suit, a white shirt and tie. After prepping for the shoot (the makeup wasn't pancake, but close to it) I pretended to exude the confidence and regal sophistication that would bode respect for my magnificent ensemble. Though I hadn't worn a suit as an actual item of fashion for a long time, I immediately tried to think of that time as a reference point to make myself feel comfortable and natural. Unfortunately, the memories were not good.

I was bereft as I sat on a stool, stretched to the ends of my psychological and emotional limits, torn between the conflict of this new life I had been trying desperately to create and renewed thoughts of my abandoned life. In disgust, I reminded myself that I had an MBA and that I had recently worked for one of the top computer giants in the world. I relented a bit and clenched my jaw; I squinted and tried again to exude the regal feeling that had been successful in prior tests. But I was tired and it showed.

After the shoot, in desperate need of companionship and empathy, if not love and acceptance, I thought of Luuk. I went right over to his apartment. I knew he didn't want any pot, but I convinced him to go with me to Thane's to buy some. Later that evening, alone together at his apartment, we decided to massage one another. Fully clothed, he sat on my back and gave me my first massage from a man. We flipped, and I gave him one back. Sitting on his back, feeling my hard-on through my pants, I was, nonetheless, far away from the fears and insecurities I had endured earlier that day. All I truly wanted was to continue to have that loving and aroused feeling. For that moment, I no longer cared about money, career, or fame. Suddenly, his brazen, loud, and super-hetero roommate burst through the doors with equally aggressive and arrogant friends. Startled, I jumped off Luuk, who also jumped up. We scrambled to the oversized chairs; with flushed faces, we pretended that nothing had happened, although it was obvious we felt we were doing something shameful. They left soon enough, but the moment was lost. Unremarkably, I later fell asleep on his couch.

The next morning—the day I was to be banned from Tokyo—we both went to Scott's, where Scott and I got high and we all three did yoga on the roof together. There against the stunning Tokyo skyline I experienced a slight moment of tranquility I often felt when doing yoga. My peacefulness was increased by doing it with the two men who stimulated me and were unafraid of what doing yoga with other men on a roof implied about their own masculinity. Later we all joined Scott's closest two friends, Stephen and Randall. Despite their overindulgence in alcohol, cocaine, and pot, which caused one to clean compulsively and the other to hide depressively in his room, they seemed to posses the secret self-knowledge I wanted. I felt they evoked an earlier classical age (both modeled high-fashion clothes and came from wealthy backgrounds). They never disclosed their sexual orientations, but neither did they talk about girlfriends or having sex with girls. As a result of this, no matter how much time I spent with them, I always left confused on some level (I wrote in my journal on September 23: "So much left said and unsaid. So much going on through secret code and veils. Is there no one I can trust?"). Nonetheless, I spent most of my remaining, sometimes idyllic, mild sunny weekends with them and with Scott, who continually fascinated me with his clever musings; "life is always grand (said with a flair) in the park; since there is only the now, we are eternal," were two of his favorites. I noted in my Franklin one weekend "the sky was blue with wispy clouds and sunshine, the trees and grass were green, and I felt warm and comfortable."

Those few fortunate moments in which I felt good about the world and myself in it ended in failed attempts at moderation. Uncontrollable drinking and using continued. In an effort to increase my seeming lack of willpower, I commanded myself to "rely on God" and to "share my faith." By the end of September, I had only succeeded in quitting smoking for two days and drinking for one prior to the start of my newest job.

The job was for a top-notch designer who I understood was named Monsieur Nicole. I was a fitting model, which meant that I was used to size the clothes the designer would use for his fashion show and in his next collection. His studio, on the outskirts of town, required that I take the subway, where I found myself feeling exceedingly tall. The walk from the subway stop was enjoyable and took me through streets and alleyways that looked oddly reminiscent of a prettier, earlier Tokyo complete with the widely spaced wooden homes, which I had envisioned prior to my arrival there.

After arriving at his tasteful, somewhat modern (for the area) facility, I was let in by a well-dressed man and told to wait. Inside, the studio consisted of one long rectangular room. There was no furniture other than one plastic and metal chair. Mirrors lined both walls and the floors were polished hardwood. Far back at the rear wall was a doorway hidden behind thick draperies. I was told to wait and did so, reading my book (most likely *The Road Less Traveled*). Shortly, the first gentleman returned with another well-dressed, more artistic man whom I thought might be Mr. Nicole, but I never clearly understood who was who. I was told to stand up and was studied while the two men murmured comments between themselves in Japanese. Neither said anything to me. Uncomfortable with being ignorant of the conversation, I was nonetheless comfortable in what I understood the job to entail. I would simply need to walk back and forth in the clothes they chose. If all went well, I might be called back or be used in their runway show, which I imagined was close to a sure thing, since all of the clothes were modeled after my body size.

The two men disappeared for a moment and then returned with an entourage of women. I was to undress down to my boxer shorts. I did as told and stood there. The large group of small women, some on their knees, dressed me completely, not allowing me to do anything myself. Together they put on the shirt and buttoned it, put my pants on, carefully zipped the fly, and pinned the hems. They buttoned my cufflinks, asked me to sit down, and put socks and shoes on my feet. I was then told to do my part and walk to the end of the room, turn around, and come back. I nervously felt an obligation to walk with confidence while simultaneously projecting a casual runway look. Returning from the far side of the room to the concentrated looks of the crowd, I was told that although I had done a good job, I did not have to worry about my walk and could be more natural. This wasn't a runway. I was relieved.

Afterward, feeling exuberant, I immediately stopped by Thane's bought hash, smoked, drank, and got high until the early hours of the morning. When told by Michiko the following day that Mr. Nicole liked me and wanted me back every week, the promise of at least one successful venture in Tokyo sadly did nothing to thwart the uncontrolled substance abuse that followed. I purchased a bottle of *Johnny Walker Red* and "got blasted," then threw up on Stephan and Randall's floor in front of Scott and Luuk. Two days later, after working a third catalog job of which I have no memory or photos, I had dinner with a model named Jack and discussed AA. I remember nothing of this, nor did I make any other notes about it. Instead, the next day, October 1, I elevated my drug use to another level.

It was both Scott's (and, coincidentally, Luuk's) last weekend in Tokyo. As a treat, Scott bought 50-plus models and their admirers LSD in the form of microdots. I later recorded every detail of what occurred in my planner. Scott was at Stephan and Randall's when I arrived that night. Together we went to Scott's drug dealer and his friend, Holden and Bip. The dealer had a 70's retro-punk apartment and matching personal style—long pink and blue hair and colorful topsiders. His friend dressed similarly, just not to such an extreme. Since being punk had only been out of style for ten years, they were either way ahead of the trendsetters who would be sporting the retro-punk look ten years hence or oddly behind the times.

Scott collected the microdots and gave me half of one, which I immediately took. We then walked to a park called Hero Park, picking up Luuk, who did not participate and wasn't much interested the whole event. The park contained small wooden bridges joining plots of land between tiny manmade lakes. The center courtyard embraced large trees on all four corners that separated paths. Though somewhat gritty by daylight, in the evening, its well-composed elements came together to create an enchanting space. The microdot had an immediate effect that built as I spent more time there.

At first, I hung out with Scott, Holden, and Bip. The dealers left soon thereafter, and Scott, who was the center of attention, quickly floated off too. Luuk had disappeared almost at once. I was left with

Rasmus, a Norwegian model, whom I had briefly met before at some weekend festivities Scott, his gang, and I participated in. Rasmus was effeminate in gesture, which turned me off. My presumption had been that men who compromised their heterosexuality risked losing their masculine traits and features, of which Rasmus seemed to me to be the perfect example. His being an occasional part of our group annoyed me; I mostly disregarded him as a non-entity.

More people left, going off on their acid trip to other parts of Tokyo. I remained, not sure where to go, as the acid continued to vibrate my mind. At one point I distinctly recall seeing the large, solid oak trees (which were too big to move in the slight breeze) throb and purposefully move their branches, with the individuality of people, much as I imagined trees of an enchanted forest did. Eventually, I agreed to leave with Rasmus to meet Michiko and the other bookers from my agency, who were having a celebration at the Lexington Queen. This wasn't necessarily a good idea. But when using, functioning at all made me irrationally think that I was functioning capably.

At first Randall, Scott and Luuk were there, but soon left. I noted in my Franklin that I said goodbye to them one at a time. Again, I lost the ability to decide it was time for me to leave. Instead I remained convinced that I needed to continually prove to my bosses, the world, and myself that I was "okay." Eventually, with only my bookers and Rasmus to talk to, I finally decided to leave as well. I knew I would find Scott at Randall and Stephan's apartment because they had mentioned earlier that they preferred to trip among themselves. Wandering out of the bar, I entered the throngs of other partiers on the sidewalk.

Despite the drug's continued potency, I clearly remember the situations that occurred and wrote the details down later. Walking on the sidewalks of the Roppongi district, I made eye contact briefly with a Japanese woman. During that brief moment I felt as if I were looking within her very soul and that I saw all her beauty. I continued walking beyond the raucous neighborhoods of central Roppongi and into the seedier bar areas where the U.S. military hung out, fearing I would be accosted on my way to where I thought the apartment was. I luckily found it without confrontation.

Once there we went up to the roof, laid on what looked like concrete burial vaults, smoked hash, talked, laughed, and looked at the near-full moon, which appeared red from the reflection of the neon lights below. It welled and wavered with the movement of hot air into the cooler air above. The clouds, too, were living, breathing, speaking entities, as was the wiggling warmth of the night. Still up at 4:30 a.m., we shared the last half of the microdot three ways (Scott had disappeared by then), drank beer, ate chips, and watched the sunrise. When Scott returned with one last ecstasy, we ground up the acid and all snorted a fourth each. I left at 10 a.m. to clean myself (and the apartment) and say goodbye to my roommate Tom. Interestingly, it was his last day too. He hadn't been invited to the drug fest, and I had spent much of my time ignoring or away from him. Desperate not to be left out of the continuing party, I quickly returned to Stephan and Randall, and we experienced our last and final (supposedly) "beautiful, clear, sunny, fresh, cool-to-warm-to-cool, breezy, perfect-buzz day at the park." In reality, I spent a portion of this time not playing Frisbee golf with the rest of the guys, which left me sitting with the effeminate Rasmus. It wasn't until Luuk called their apartment, where we had returned much later, that I was once again rescued from myself and taken home. There in my apartment, my quiet, sensitive, Belgian friend nursed me down with a glass of *Cutty Sark* and two cigarettes. He left me to crash alone at 10 p.m. and then patiently gathered me together the next day—his last. After buying me a banana crepe and coffee, he walked with me to buy the hash I so desperately needed to ease my recovery. He then spent his last hour hanging out with me while I smoked it before he left. Though we would keep in touch and I would think of him kindly, when the opportunity arose for us to cross paths again, I wrote him off as a friend because I feared he wouldn't accept my true nature.

SexNoCum4Me 11

Journal: 2:42 AM - Tuesday October 5, Tokyo-Akasaka-Roppongi: *I've been meaning to write for days now. So much concerns me. So much is so good and so bad. The wind can blow quickly in any direction. I basically have no money and a lot of possessions. I'm a free spirit still though evil lurks in every corner and there are signs every day and many hours. The people I'm dying to be with are distant and always somehow disappointing. What am I looking for? Perfect people in such an imperfect world? I feel not a part of this society for sure and long for the comforts of beauty around me in nature and serenity. I miss serenity. I miss any semblance of order. I'm afraid I'm becoming more like the lost, more like the chaos than changing it. It is too much to change alone or even make much of an impression.*

I'm afraid of losing my soul to it and disgusted by that thought. I feel a failure in the business world. I feel a failure in the world of comfortable quiet middle to upper-middle class home values and attracted to the chaotic come what will nomadic hippy lifestyle of modeling. I want more from myself. So much more I want to be aware and giving and capable of giving. I don't want to be so wrapped up or lost in the scene that I become one of the many. I don't know what I'm looking for or what to do with what I find other than build a better model. But a model should be a model inside and out I can't just let everything go for the joy of the moment. Am I a loner with no real ties? Aren't we all.

Will this bring me down or up in the long run. Can I refrain, sustain, maintain, explain, and rize or will I fall in utter, annihilation, humiliation, poverty and ruin? Somehow I hope for the best although I don't feel the best is here. Maybe tomorrow. I am without blame except for my sarcasm, my anger and my chronic urge to entertain and be entertained. Everyone looks to me to either pass up or drink the next drink. I am truly the star and the movie changes with my every move good or bad. I pray it leads to good and freedom.

My new roommate Gerrick moved in and I was informed by the

104

agency that he, although much newer to Tokyo than me, had qualified for Tom's bigger room, which aggrieved me greatly. Gerrick was 22, from the South like Sean, was with Ugly in Milan, and Ford in New York—agencies that I knew made him a top model. His composite card portrayed him looking dashing in a jacket and naïvely playful in casual wear, with lips slightly pursed as if waiting for a kiss to bring him out of his sullen reverie.

Being subjected to my shitty room while the new guy got the better one with a view gave me another excuse to be mad at Michiko. My housing problems also continued back in the States. A call to my San Diego credit union revealed that I was one month behind on my mortgage payment, but the bank was willing to renegotiate—the California real-estate market was sinking just in time for me to tank on my obligations to pay the mortgage. I still had barely enough money to survive in Tokyo let alone make any mortgage payments at all. I reconciled this by a belief that if I got the next big casting, for a big Toyota casting was promising thousands, I'd have the money I needed, overnight.

Ading to my list of concerns was that my time would soon be ending in Japan, which meant I needed to think about where I would go and what I might do. Marketing myself around the world in an extremely fickle industry as a physical commodity with limited information was not very easy. But I was no longer capable of working a normal job, and I had hoped to make better of my investment in my new career. I debated returning to Milan, where at least I thought I had money in the bank (from the Hugo Boss show), or to go into other markets. Luuk was eventually going to Brazil. But I heard that even though I could get tear sheets and have a lot of fun there, it didn't pay well. Although accumulating photos while not making any money and partying a lot was what I actually did, it wasn't my mindset to plan actively to do this. Osaka, a secondary market to Tokyo, was nearby, but there wasn't much full-time work there. I also heard of and knew models who went to Israel, Korea, or Thailand and were happy and successful, although rumor was that some disappeared into the jungle in the latter two countries.

The Detroit area, where my mom lived and wanted me to return, and where I could get financial support until I got my feet back on the ground, was a last resort. This would mean moving back to the state I had escaped six years before, when I moved to San Diego. Two years before moving to San Diego I had also moved out of Detroit, but then returned. I had failed at my first post-college job at the Palmer House in Chicago. I was also running away from the gay men I met there. If, as a 22-year-old, I had remained in Chicago, I would have had to face my fears. I couldn't, so I returned to Michigan where I lived with my father in the upscale community of Troy. I knew that another return to Michigan and the arms of my loving mother and grandmother (my dad died during the time I lived with him) would most likely result in the same lackluster stasis in my personal development that the last return had (although I was able to make peace with my dad before he died). It would also symbolize that I had failed in all the career, money, and life objectives I left Michigan to seek. Besides, working in a modeling agency there meant traveling around the country to spin on platforms for auto-shows or a return to corporate America.

Although the decisions were hard, and I felt alone in making them, trying to figure out what I thought Jesus wanted was harder for me still. And doing all the above while stoned and drunk was nearly impossible. Despite all of this, I did feel that I was making progress. I wrote in my journal: "I owe Japan for helping me to grow up; become a man; somewhere in-between." And the following shortly thereafter: **Journal, Thursday, October 7**: *I've come to grips today with my own heterosexuality and homosexuality. Awoke to [forced] masturbated thoughts with women. Closed the day with unspoken understanding in a beautiful friend - Randall. Surviving and growing in a world fraught with subliminal and oh so subtle homo and bisexuality. The movements and eye contacts. Yet everyone wants to be accepted [and all are] working through layers of our own shit in this medium or environment of super hype, performance and specialness. Who are we? We're all the*

106

same yet very different. So much is transacted and communicated non-verbally and ever so slight as to be completely invisible. Our own desires and hopes and dreams mesh with everyone around us on some sort of trip. We're all paranoid and of the same things because it's inside of us as well as around us. I feel luckier than others. For what reason I'm not sure. Hidden in Japan…So far away yet so near.

On a cool, rainy day I noted as "the day of 100,000 umbrellas," I finished that day's work for Mr. Nicole. After being touched and viewed for money that I knew would pay off debt but not find its way into my pocket, I pitched in for a bottle of Absolut with Randall and Steve. Randall disappeared at some point. I went out to look for him at the Lexington Queen and found Rasmus instead. Feeling uncomfortable, I wondered what others might think if they caught me sitting alone and talking to him. I don't remember if Rasmus bought me a drink, but I didn't record spending any money on one. Early in the morning, we finally left the bar and went back to my apartment, where I had hoped to find the vending machine still open for the night, as well as some pot. I told Rasmus to be quiet as we entered the apartment, because Gerrick was, as usual, asleep early due to his heavy work schedule. We conversed only briefly before I let Rasmus undo my pants, get down on his knees, and suck me from my squeaky, flat bed. I remember a further image of me lying on the mottled, shag, dirty carpet, my pants wrapped around my ankles, in a 69 position. I didn't come, as I not so eloquently scribbled in the far, hidden corner of my Franklin, "Sex – no cum 4 me." I have no memory of how he felt or if he came.

Terrorized that someone might discover us, I firmly instructed Rasmus to shut the door quietly as he left. He responded by slamming it as hard as he could. The metal reverberated against the concrete stairwell so hard I could hear it echo. I wrote in my journal to calm down. At first, I wrote about "intelligent eyes and hands touching my body and the fabric over my skin," which represented the fit modeling work I did earlier the previous day. I then wrote "the key to controlling drinking is to have a high tolerance and not increase use." As I continued, random thoughts became coherent to the point where

I finally admitted to myself that I might be gayer than I had previously thought. Months before, in the presence of my therapist, when I was struggling to stay honestly sober in San Diego, I allowed that perhaps I was 10% gay and 90% straight. That night in Tokyo, I wrote "…34% gay and 66% straight" in my journal based upon a formula of Scott's, which may have represented what he concluded himself to be.

The next morning Steve and Randall left. On their way out, they came by my sex pad and drug warren and woke me up with the remainder of a bottle of vodka. Drinking vodka in the aesthetics of my apartment shed light on how unsophisticated the act seemed to me there. I couldn't comprehend how Sean and Tom did it so frequently. They didn't have the sensibilities I imagined we had. We drank the little left, and then I went for a walk alone in the cemetery.

Conversations with Lothar, Luuk, my Catholic girlfriends, and Linda, my college friend, made me think that cemeteries were cool and a great place to go for solitude to think about life and death. The one in central Tokyo was different from any I had known. Instead of tombstones, there were enormous monoliths jutting up from parcels of land like a setting on a far-away planet. Finding the cemetery remote, I returned home.

The following day was a Sunday, my favorite day to get fucked-up. Sunday had traditionally been a day that I sometimes went to church and sometimes took communion. Having done either or both, I left thinking that I had cleansed my body and soul of impurities and thus had a clean slate. Additionally, I believed that since I was not beholden to an employer on Sunday I owed it to myself to drink as hard as I would on a Friday or Saturday (this didn't take into account the fact that I smoked or drank whenever, anyhow). Nothing had changed my rationale about excessive substance abuse that Sunday despite not going to church or my lack of a 9-to-5 job.

Enthusiastically, I participated in doing the microdots that had become such a hit in Tokyo with my new roommate Gerrick, a female friend of his, Anna Lee, and Sean, in celebration of his leaving, which was to be the next day. Anna Lee was a beautiful, young girl who also was a Southerner like Gerrick and Sean. She had a flock of gorgeous girlfriends who soon became my acquaintances and who sponsored my partying the last weekend of my stay. She, like many others, though well represented with great agencies, probably found herself in Tokyo because she was extremely petite. Despite the fact that Gerrick had a girlfriend back home and Anna Lee had a boyfriend, they both engaged in exploring a little more than just a friendship in Tokyo. Everyone agreed to my exuberant idea.

Sean and I went to Thor's to buy the microdots and hash. Once there, Sean popped an entire pill. I waited for Gerrick and Anna Lee to divide the remaining. The acid took its affect, but less so than the first time. We began our trip by wandering around Tokyo and visiting my old friend Bram. The absinthe days were child's play, but we did smoke some hash, and shortly ditched him. Hoping for a replay of the moon experience, I took our group to the rooftop of the building where Randall and Stephan had lived. But the moon wasn't full, and the event had lost its charm. Feeling nothing special, we decided to buy two more microdots and some more hash that Anna Lee paid for.

Back at our apartment, I took photos as we bantered about, laughing, holing up in corners, and saying goodbye to Sean. Anna Lee, Gerrick, and I then lay around the floor. At times, we got beers from the vending machine and took periodic valiums. At one point, we stood in a circle, the three of us with our heads connected and our hands mingled. I felt, and the others concurred, that we all felt at that moment as one. No one knew whose head or finger's were whose. All of the fingers were all of *our* fingers, and we were each inside each other's head. The fingers then became waves of writhing, wiggling, moist, flesh. And then they became the cigarettes in the ashtray, of which I noted in my Franklin we had smoked 20 packs.

For a time, the sensuality of the three of us together was wonderful—reminiscent of my graduate school days when my best two friends (one male and one female) and I spent every waking moment together. I may have kissed Anna Lee briefly and moved to kiss Gerrick. But then Anna Lee and Gerrick started making out. I felt left out just as I had in my earlier experience when my two best friends became a couple. Having been drunk and stoned through the prior episode—never fully, consciously experiencing its depth—I continued to dwell in it as if it were still repeating itself. I decided to leave, feeling as confused as I had in the past.

I walked over to new acquaintances, both late-teenage girls. I told them my entire life's experiences with sexuality. I then walked to the police box to make my Sunday call to my mother. Unfortunately, I was stopped by police officers, and almost was arrested—most likely for my illegal phone cards. I made a dash straight back home, where I was glad to be back in the company of Gerrick and Anna Lee, who were still hanging out in the apartment wondering where I had gone. We smoked another bowl together and I noted that we bonded again. I nonetheless went to sleep feeling "pissed" at them.

The next day began a deeper level of questioning that continued for the rest of my stay in Tokyo: "I live on the opposite end of the world, where everything goes, I want to do everything…but I, as a Christian, did serious acid, valiums, cigarettes, hash and had homo sex—God, why am I such a bad egg?" I wrote. "Will I ever stop?" I continued. "How can non-religious people like Gerrick have such appreciation for everything?…Why do I lack it?…Why do I get smiles from Japanese people even when I am in the midst of questioning my faith for Jesus?…Is modeling really my calling?…Why then is it so difficult for me?…Do I need to grovel in order to do God's will?" I followed these questions with a list of wants, some of which exhibited a spiritual maturing well beyond what seemed probable for me at the time: "…love, to win every now and then, expressive freedom, wisdom/knowledge," and "to have spiritual peace."

Many times, I had prayed that God kill me if I ever lost my faith in Jesus. But increasingly I felt that belief seemed at odds with my knowledge that my feelings for men were not going to go away.

That afternoon, I got on my hands and knees, confessed to being a Christian and prayed for death in my sleep if that was God's will for me. At 2 a.m. I took a walk alone in the cemetery. Illuminated by the lights of the city all around it, the cemetery was clearly empty, the wind blew, and it was cold. Frightened, I quickly walked through it and home. The next morning having not been smitten by God, I resolved that I wanted the dream and was willing to pay the price for it even if it meant sleeping in a train station. I was happy that everything happened for a reason—even my leaving Tokyo in poverty—and excited to go back to Germany and Milan. "NEW LIFE BEGINS!" I wrote in capital letters in my Franklin.

I went to the agency to retrieve the copy of my book that they— and all agencies—kept for clients to view, and to talk with Michiko. I was told I would receive $150 on Friday, along with my return plane ticket to Munich. This would be my complete payout, which was more than contractually what was due me, given the fact that I hadn't worked the prerequisite number of jobs. I knew the money would have to pay the exit tax at the airport, the shuttle (if it hadn't already been paid for) and all transportation to get me to Milan from the Munich airport.

I worked my job for Mr. Nicole. It was during either this job or the prior one that I realized I had mistaken Mr. Nicole to be a person, when in actuality Monsieur Nicole was the line designed by the famous Japanese designer Yukio Kobayashi, for the Matsuda menswear collection. There was no Mr. Nicole, and I have no idea if I ever met Mr. Kobayashi. I also found out I would not be used in the fashion show later in Paris.

I spent my last weekend in a drunken binge on the town with a host of acquaintances. I would feel the same superficial attachment I did for my high school graduating class (and would likewise never hear from, see, or think about again). Thor the drug dealer got me stoned, the owner of Spirals got me drunk, a bevy of teenage girls took me out to dinner, and Anna Lee and her beautiful friends got me high on a quarter tab of ecstasy—too weak to freak me out but strong enough to keep me going until I closed the bars. The new group of young girls had grown in sophistication from the old days of two months before. The ecstasy now came from a tall, black dealer who wore a top hat and frequented the popular clubs. When requested, he produced whatever the pretty girls wanted—hash, microdots, heroin, cocaine, or, in our case, ecstasy—from the elastic of his hatband.

On my last day one of my new, young girlfriends and I went for one last walk through the cemetery to clear my mind and soul. As usual, we walked by endless large pillars we did not understand. We both fell silent, wondering at how different it all seemed. As we continued our wandering, we came across a Christian section. There was what appeared to be an entire community all with similar dates of demise dating from the early part of the last century. It was as if the entire Christian community had been wiped out. We found a statue of Mary, which seemed particularly ominous. About her feet were serpents that looked up at her face. It seemed to me they also worked their way up her body. Did other Mary statues look like this, I wondered. If not, what atrocity could be happening to this Mary in Tokyo?

The following afternoon, with my approximate $150 from the agency, $26 from my prior savings, and 1 DM from my German money, I walked to a hotel where I waited for the shuttle. Nervously I rode to the airport hoping I had enough money to pay for the shuttle and the exit tax. I knew I didn't have the strength to figure out how to survive in Tokyo any longer. But I also felt confident that something was looking out for me. It had to be. To my good fortune, the shuttle cost a minimal $30, and the exit tax was only $20. I now had to fly to Frankfurt, switch flights to Munich, figure out some way to get to Milan, and try to get to the money from my account with Ugly People. If I were still lucky, I'd also find a place to live.

Portfolio

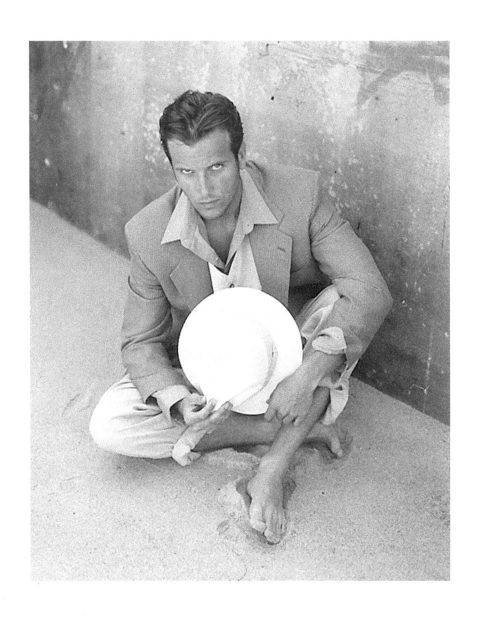

the most successful test in L.A. before the trip

second photo shoot in Milan: abandoned church grounds

Milan photo shoot using pants as a turbin

first photo shoot in Milan

KRIZIAUOMO
Flanella gessata per il blazer

first job: <u>Max</u>

119

photo shoot with Hobbes

ロイヤルブランドの
エレガンス、
ムッシュ君島を
着こなす。

吉田弘明 ●写真
Photo by Hiroaki Yoshida
Styling by LID*
Masanobu Nao, Hideho Kozono,
Satoshi Yoda
Hair by Yoshie Sugiyama (CLIP)
Model: Robert

ムッシュ君島 ●協力
Phone: 03-3291-2311

ゆったりとしたラインが大人っぽさを醸し出
す。そろそろエレガントを考えてもいい年相
を持ちたいものだ。ジャケット 10万円、シャ
ツ 1万4000円、コート 9万3000円、タイ 1万
円、パンツ 4万5000円

november 1993 **MEN'S EXTRA** 128

Men's Extra in Tokyo

121

Ph. Oliviero Toscani

Ricerche di ENRICO COVERI

Enrico Coveri:
appeared in American <u>GQ</u>

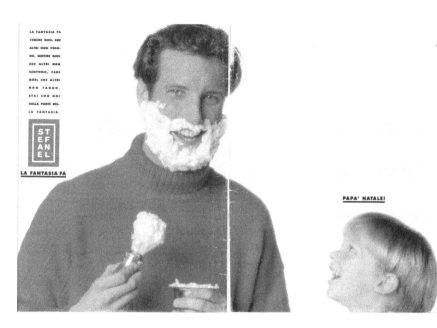

Father Christmas ad

Fendi show photo

Primera hora de la mañana. El hombre más clásico lleva pijama a rayas marino, gris y granate, muy holgado, con chaqueta con cuello, realizado en algodón cien por cien. Es un diseño de Adolfo Domínguez. Las gafas graduadas son del creador italiano Giorgio Armani.

El Pais

124

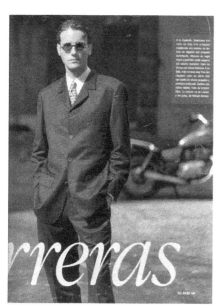

Nenunco ad in Madrid

San Diego, 1994:
test shoot

Paris

YouLookMaavelous 12

Our first meal on the Tokyo-to-Frankfurt flight was sushi. Halfway through the flight the menu switched to sausage and sauerkraut, to the dismay of the Japanese passengers. As the plane got nearer to Germany, my anxiety also began to rise. I would need to transfer in Frankfurt to a Munich flight. I wondered what awaited me. To go on to Milan, I'd have to get to the train station, and then be able to afford a ticket. In the meantime, I'd have to eat. My money had dwindled to approximately $100—100 times less than what I originally thought I'd have. Who knew when I'd be able to access the million lire (approximately $600) I hoped was in the Ugly vault as payment for the Hugo Boss show. And then I'd need to pay a deposit to live somewhere. Despite my earlier fears of him, Hobbes now seemed to be the one with the answers.

Upon my layover in Frankfurt, I eyed a bin of bananas. I quickly took several, stuffing them into the bag that contained the rest of my worldly possessions. The connecting flight landed in Munich at what would have been 7:30 a.m. Tokyo time—past even my bedtime. But I had farther to go. I made it to the train station where I stood in line nervously. I reached the ticket counter. The ticket girl was sweet as I smiled, flirted, and told her that I had a little bit of money with which to get to Milan. She rang up the ticket for the price of a minor passenger, which accurately summed up my emotional condition. It cost 68 DM, which along with a pack of cigarettes, was all I had.

The overnight train was harrowing. At both the Swiss and Italian borders, security personnel entered the sleeping compartments. Because I was sleeping on the top bunk, I was unmolested by the German shepherds that came through to sniff out illegal drugs. Luckily, I had none with me, and I had washed my clothes before the trip.

Even though I survived the dogs, I felt antsy in my skin, withdrawing from the alcohol and drugs that had helped make Tokyo such a strange experience.

I assume I jumped the subway turnstile once I landed in Milan. Bedraggled, hungry, tired, malnourished, and impoverished, I reached Ugly People just as Hobbes was opening up. He let me in and looked me over. "You look maavelous" he said, "Tokyo was good for you." Indeed, the emaciated, pale, addict-look was very much *in* for the fall season.

I immediately went upstairs to wait for the accountants to give me a check for some of my money. There, the elaborate metal bars I stood behind were designed to look imposing rather than to keep anybody out. This check and future ones I then cashed at a different bank. Regardless of which one I visited, I still received the same steely, unfriendly glances. It appeared that no one was happy to pay out money, especially to models without working visas.

Fortunately, Hobbes had also set me up in a good living situation. My new residence was the Hotel Odescalchi—a big step up from the Giusti. I had two roommates. One was a gorgeous Dutch model named Gregor, and the other was an effeminate boy whom I innately disliked and ignored, and whose late-nights and partying (though he didn't party in the room and was rarely there) annoyed Gregor (simply because Gregor had a serious respect for our occupation). Gregor had a square, chiseled face, deep, penetrating brown eyes, a solid frame, and luscious, thick lips. He also was married, which made him seem "safe" and available to be my friend. He immediately became the perfect replacement for Scott, Luuk and nameless other guys through the years back to grade school whom I adored, loved, and secretly lusted after.

Gregor's bed and mine formed an L-shape at the end of the rectangular studio. Our heads rested only a few feet apart. I heard and smelled him as he awoke in the middle of the night to smoke a cigarette. I sat up and did the same. Sitting in the dark, we talked about our lives and fears before going back to sleep. I liked how

130

Gregor did pushups and went to bed every night at 10:45 p.m. My looking at a newspaper clipping of a marine doing pushups led to my first experience masturbating, and now I was doing pushups in my bedroom before bedtime with my new best friend and sexy roommate. This simple activity was stimulating on many levels.

Being proudly Dutch, Gregor was also a pothead—I would soon discover that he smoked more hash than anyone I ever knew—which he considered was a daily necessity much like drinking water. But my first night with him I neither drank alcohol nor did drugs and proudly wrote this on a half page in my Franklin surrounded by a big square. I knew, as usual, that I *needed* to be clear-headed, but this time, after fucking up so badly in Tokyo, I felt it was even more important. The elimination of ecstasy, microdots, grain alcohol, absinthe, and, in fact, most alcohol, surely was beneficial. Adding to this comparative sobriety was a newly formed, co-dependent adherence to Gregor's better-than-average discipline, responsibility, and consistent schedule (when to eat, when to sleep, when to get up, etc.).

Gregor was also with Ugly People, which is why Hobbes knew that he needed a roommate. Unfortunately, he didn't think Ugly was doing enough for him and wanted to leave. Despite only being back for one day, and having Hobbes find me a place to stay and keep me on, I felt that Gregor was right. After all, what had Hobbes done for me? Gregor, who was quite successful in Milan and Paris and hung out with even more successful models (one of the most successful models in the world was his best friend), felt that I had a good look. This was enough for me to feel confident in my ability to do better.

Within two days of my return, we scouted out new agencies and looked forward to the possibility of getting the same one. The agency we visited that day, Eye-For-Eye—an appropriate name to hoist our revenge on Hobbes—was successful for Gregor but not for me. Upon our return to Ugly, Gregor had "a major blowout" with Hobbes and Hobbes' booker Antonella. Deciding that he now wanted to retrieve his second book—the book kept at the agency to be used to submit to clients who wanted to see more—I agreed to create a diversion. Apparently, I bizarrely screamed "fuck" twenty times while Gregor stole his second book from the cabinet where he knew Hobbes kept them.

The following day would be my turn. We both went to an agency called Beatrice (pronounced Be-ah-tree-chay) where one by one we handed our books to the agents. Given that Gregor and I had come together and he was so accomplished, I was allowed to sit around the circular booking table and chat with the five female bookers as they took turns looking at my book. After a short and cordial chat during which I was extremely self-conscious, I was relieved to sit in the waiting area while they continued to peruse my book and talk among themselves. To calm my unfettered nerves, I opened my Franklin and scribbled down my anxieties. Shortly thereafter, to my great relief, they told me they liked me.

I'm not sure if Gregor was accepted or not, but know that he made a professional choice to go to Eye-for-Eye. That day and the next, as was instructed, I sat around my new agency. There wasn't anything to be said, so I looked at the second copies of the books they had for other models and listened to the five women work at the big round desk that reminded me of the set-up I had seen in Paris. Eventually they sent me to a casting for an entire campaign—billboards, magazine ads, and catalogues—for Baldassarini (I had forgotten that Baldassarini was the sophisticated new line of Hugo Boss clothing introduced at the show I had worked in Cologne). Friday, I got an urgent call—I would be working on Monday. I had been awarded the campaign, which was a great accomplishment for any model.

A blissful weekend with Gregor followed. Saturday we sunned in the park and walked to the beautiful centerpiece of Milan, the medieval church known as the Duomo. I later watched him steal a can of coffee from a small food market, wondering why anyone would do such a thing, but not judging him for it. It began to rain that evening, so we stayed in. I wrote a long and overly idealistic mass letter to all my friends telling them I would be home for Christmas before I again left for Paris. I called my grandmother who was sick with grief for me. After dispensing half-truths and fantasies to my friends and family, and after Gregor went to bed, I tried to be honest with myself in my journal.

Journal October 23: *I'm somehow surrounded by people yet very lonely still. [Our other roommate] is off to some bar somewhere with a big group of people and Gregor has gone to bed. It's midnight - Saturday night. Who am I? I should be farther along - should have started earlier. Everyone respects me tremendously and I'm so full of self-doubt, still-mixed with arrogance. I wish and I hope I have the strength of character to make my own decisions. Now its time to really keep focused in myself, to stay away from drugs and to not be distracted by the model scene, the free booze, drugs and chaos of being in a room full of people I don't know and many of whom I will never see again. I despise the social scene though it is very much a very important part of this reality. I want to go home to take care of business but must also take care of business here first so that I can afford to go home.*

I feel well rested after a week of good normal sleep. To bed at reasonable hour, up early and busy doing things all day I want to and will cut down on smoking and drugs and heavy drinking I already know are no no's for me. I feel I have yet, another in the zillions of chances I've had and I can't fuck up this time. Two months behind on mortgage payments, the place not rented out yet. What's next? Bankruptcy. The loneliness persists, my hands shake and I wonder if I'll ever be loved. The key lies in not needing to be liked by everyone, and loving myself more. I know that but it doesn't come naturally. So I have to constantly think I'm okay. I'm surviving against incredible odds of my own personality and the almost impossible situation around me.

Sunday, our last day as roommates, we spent another idyllic day together. We walked to the outdoor market, watched boys play soccer, played video games, hung out in a café where we had a sandwich and cappuccino, and went to the end of mass in the Duomo. Gregor scared away men he claimed were thieves from out front of the church, which I found ironic, considering his earlier thievery. That night I invited him

133

to participate in some yoga on the floor after our customary pushups. I wanted to experience the type of companionship I felt with Luuk and Scott on the roof in Tokyo. But this was not to be. He declined, sat on his bed, and read the paper. The following morning he left, but I would soon see him again.

The job for Baldassarini was for both Monday and Tuesday. The shoot used black and white film to add a classic touch. I worked with a beautiful Belgian female named Anais. Unfortunately, the clothes were once again too large for me, so the photographer tried to shoot close-ups of her and me in seductive poses. Instead of feeling sexual, I felt and looked terrorized. The photographer shouted at me in frustration to hold her, to pull her close to me, to get into it. Anais did her part by posing in sexual, kissing gestures while I stood there clueless, her hand around my throat, hoping that the photographer would just take the damn pictures.

After our second day of shooting, I imagined I had fallen in love with Annais as we sipped a cappuccino in a nearby bistro. While eating croissants, I convinced myself she wanted me, and would, at any moment, either kiss me or invite me on a date. She, in turn, only wanted to converse, and gave me two sentimental kisses on the cheek as she left. Feeling emotionally drained from the shoot and rejected by Annais, I consoled myself by thinking I, like many a heroic straight man, had been shunned. I eventually learned that the shoot was a failure for the client too, and had to be reshot—a fact I learned after I was accidentally called back to the reshoot casting.

The following day, October 27, was my thirtieth birthday, which I noted in my Franklin as "the start of my new life." To celebrate I decided it was time to live alone—away from the two roommates (one new) who I felt annoyed at and saddened by since neither were Gregor. I moved down the hall where I would have my own space for the first time since I left San Diego. I took two baths: one in which I recorded that I baptized myself "in the name of the Father, Son and Holy Ghost." I listened to inspirational songs by U2 and Lenny Kravitz, drank a bottle of champagne, smoked hash, and ate well (a lima bean, garlic, olive oil, tomato, and beet salad with pasta with tomatoes, zucchini, onions, mushrooms, and garlic sauce). I scribbled in my journal that, like the song Lenny Kravitz sang, I believed in myself. And somehow, I realized "I Am That I Am," the greatest statement that any of us make, to confirm our self-worth and to recognize that we are a part of God and, therefore, *are* God. I then walked to the discount-clothing store and bought some reasonably priced shirts. I felt my grandmother would be happy with the prudence I used in spending my $100 in birthday money she had deposited to my account in the States. As night fell, I walked outside and looked up to find a huge, nearly full, bright orange moon.

In the days that followed my addictions reached stasis, my modeling became more successful, and my emotional conflicts reemerged. Although Gregor lived elsewhere, our friendship continued and we smoked copious amounts of hash together. As the bond of brotherly love blurred to sexual moments of arousal by me, I grew more paranoid that he might think I was gay while I tried to suppress any gesture, facial movement, or inflection that would give myself away (to him or to me). For his part, Gregor remained a sympathetic, conversant friend, never badgering me with the idle male model exercise of girl talk. Instead he remained supportive, complementing me on how my career was doing and remarking on how much more it seemed I would soon work compared to him.

Aurora was also in Milan, and I re-engaged in my stoned and frustrating relationship with her. I never resolved my lack of lust for her with what I expected of myself, thereby always feeling impotent, fearful, and, ironically, *used* for my sympathy, instead of my body. For her part, Aurora loved me as much as she was capable of caring. Oddly, we reminisced about the good times we had at the Giusti, and once went to visit the live-in switchboard operator, Giovanni, both leaving with the feeling that we no longer belonged there. She loaned me a book, some incense, a few candles, and Simon & Garfunkle and

135

Van Morrison tapes so that I could have nice evenings of bath taking. Recognizing that the gigantic pimples that were breaking out all over my face were something she suffered from too, she suggested a great remedy: stick my head over a pan of steaming water and cover the whole thing with a towel.

Spiritually, Aurora believed that we are all one, which I thought was nice but not enough. I told her that I felt it was my mission in the modeling industry "to bring good to people and to promote sobriety," which I understood myself to practice (!!). Secretly, I also felt it was my job to save her soul through Jesus. In the meantime, we spent hours supporting each other's hash habit. As with my drinking, I mostly held onto the threadbare idea that the problem with me getting it on with Aurora and therefore being straight was outside of me. I needed a woman that was "pretty, intelligent, strong, stylish, self-aware and not gaudy, pretentious, or unladylike." After my job with Anais, I decided that French women were the most "sexy, interesting, and stylish."

Journal November 12: *When I'm with Aurora as I was tonight, I feel mixed emotions. Like she's a great friend or something. Tonight she said I'm a good candidate for an ulcer. And she had her feet barely touching my leg. I tried to maintain cool, and not flinch. The feelings I get aren't sexual maybe even more threatened to withhold any sort of facial expression that won't represent terror (fear or mush puppy love expressions). I basically recommended a psychotherapist to her today. I think she has a lot of anger towards men (father, brother perhaps, definitely past boyfriend's who fucked her over big time) and also a drive for some sort of direction for her lost or not clear spirituality. I'm inept, impotent, and imbecilic - all of which <u>really are false</u>. All of this creates so much stress and confusion that the last thing seems to be intimacy although that is what I really need, have been searching for and do <u>want</u>.*

My San Diego financial sinkholes exacerbated any minor sense of financial well being I could muster. During the first day of the Baldassarini job, I had the unpleasant news that my condo payments had moved into collections. My birthday money back home went to pay for my phone card and items my mother felt were necessary (like the renter's insurance I needed to cover my lost Hugo Boss camcorder, and, of all things, the San Diego Gas and Electric utility bill that, in her confusion, she thought was important to pay). I couldn't help but continually question whether I had made a good choice about coming to Europe. I wrote in my journal "I feel good about $5,800 in total modeling earnings to date and less than $4,000 in direct modeling costs" (research and development), and that "I am an entrepreneur now, an entrepreneur with a lot of debt." I recognized that I had to move again, and found someone—a 19 year-old named Spartan, whom I don't remember—to share a less expensive room in one of the coolest residential hotels in the city, the Darcena.

Luckily, I soon worked my second extremely impressive job— a campaign for Stefanel, a major clothing line. I would appear on billboards and newspaper ads all over Italy. I showed up at the shoot expecting high fashion and was surprised. Instead of high fashion, I was made to wear a simple red sweater. Instead of make-up, I was told to lather shaving cream on my face. My shaggy hair was combed back, and I was handed a razor. The next thing I knew, a young boy stood next to me and I was asked to smile. I was to be Father Christmas—the giver of gifts—and a dad. I smiled as instructed and laughed along with the farce. I worked with the boy as best as I could. When it was all over, I went back to the apartment and toasted my "midlife crisis" with my teenage roommate.

The following day I met Cameron, a well-known test photographer in Milan who had been there many times before. He was also the test photographer who had taken the successful shoots of me in Los Angeles before I left for Europe. He and his girlfriend Melissa had moved out of Beverly Hills and were now living in a small apartment, but wanted to live in the Darcena. They knew of a large room there with a separate bedroom, large, comfortable, fully furnished living room, and a real kitchen and dinette. Rent was steep, Cameron was still working at making it, and Milan wasn't a very generous city when it came to paying anyone. They needed my help as a roommate to swing it. I had $1,000, which I equated either with a ticket back to the states, or 22 days' rent with Cameron and Melissa. I later wrote in my journal "I need faith that my basic needs are met" and that Friday, November 12, moved with Cameron and his girlfriend into a nicer apartment on the third floor of the same hotel residence where I had been living.

Once there, I had the opportunity to experience models coming to the apartment to shoot tests and check out Cameron's book. One of those models was my friend Gregor. Gregor came over early on Saturday—he was always an early riser—and Melissa made us potatoes for breakfast served with powerful cups of espresso. After this he and I went to a casting, then back to the apartment for more coffee—Gregor loved coffee and drank a lot of it; I knew it made me nervous but didn't care. We followed this with another casting and a walk in the park to buy some hash. It was drizzling and cold outside, and the walk in the park to buy illegal drugs seemed wonderfully romantic to me. It was, I noted, reminiscent of the time when he and I walked in the park to watch the boys play soccer—a game he adored and I tried to appreciate for him. After obtaining our purchase, we took a bus to his house, rolled two joints, drank three more cups of coffee and ate sandwiches until 9 p.m. when I left to go home. It all went well except for a visit by his good friend, the Hugo Boss campaign model Mark Vanderloo. For that short time, I felt intimidated, judged and strangely outted.

I came home paranoid and with a sweaty nose to the waiting Cameron and Melissa, whom I called Mom and Dad, who wanted to talk. The following morning we continued our discussion, which I recorded in my journal: **(Journal November 15)** *I was very heavy today. I almost felt depressed. [A male model] was being shot by Cameron - nice guy - fascinating. Later Cameron and I talked. He wanted to get straight – me. He wants to know - something. I told him that I've had experiences - one in Chicago - I did not admit or disclose the experience I had with Rasmus the Finish boy or Vova the man from Hamburg and the train and for this I feel uncomfortable. [The* *model] kept talking about being happy with oneself - ones body and who they are. Cameron, I sense, despises models although he appears friendly and conversational to them - like he's their best friend. I don't trust him fully yet, nor should I. He probably doesn't trust himself. Three days here and I don't need to tell my life story. I don't owe anyone that. I don't need to disclose my life's secrets but I shouldn't be ashamed of them either. For the most part I need to be completely honest with myself first.*

The last time I had sex with a woman was with Eve. Again, I didn't cum inside her. She just bounced on me and acted so aggressive - almost painfully - that I couldn't get off inside her. Before her was Dawn. We never fucked. The relationship soured quickly though after I started bumming on her religion and pimples - she didn't believe in medicine and was <u>way</u> too earthy for me. And then there was Lori. She was so hard I couldn't barely stick my dick in her, and so much with anger towards men and the schizophrenic family. Shannon before that. Thirteen years or so on me and multiple lives.

Before that just short affairs with women and Fin. After Eve I have had a sexual encounter with (oh, Marcus before Eve) two men, neither really fulfilling. No fulfillment with Rasmus - I couldn't and didn't cum although I felt the need to go ahead and defecate myself - why? And with Vova, masturbating together in the park - not really very exciting - not me. Drunk and hashed out. I need to sober up. The perfect woman probably doesn't exist for me out there and all those I'm really after are not the right thing for me.

I've experienced some form of sexual contact with both men and women mostly with women and more fullfillingly so…if asked I might say 66% straight and 34% gay. [This conveniently worked out to be a 70-30 ratio to the list of names (9 women and 4 men) that I had been keeping.] *So what do I want now?*

Point: As a human I need sexual gratification
Point: As a human I need companionship
Point: As a human I need friends I like and I can trust.
Point: I would like a sexual relationship with a woman
Point: I'm freaked about Aids and clinginess
Point: Life's short and I will not be here forever

Point: I doom myself to relationships with women who destroy me, my very soul, and my feelings of manliness.

Point: I need to keep my eyes open be confident (which I hope and pray will come with some success at this business) and date and have fun.

I'm not into having allsorts of wild sexual affairs.

After writing this, I began reading *Interview with a Vampire*, which I loved for its homosexual undertones—interestingly I had turned off my tape recorder to watch a Dracula movie one of the last times I was this honest with myself; that night I came out to myself about Petey. At some point, I decided to reveal more information to Cameron. I let him know about my homosexual experiences in Hamburg and Tokyo and that they were not for me. Afterwards I wrote, "No big deal; I'm free from it all; It was honest; I've shared it with God, myself and one other person; and I feel completely relieved; Amen." I had learned in my short stint with sobriety that a key to staying sober was to be thoroughly honest with myself, my Higher Power and one other person. The point, however, was that honesty came from inner-searching while being sober—drinking and drugging *less* didn't count. And it would have been preferable to discuss emotionally tumultuous issues with a trained therapist or at least someone who could help and support me. Consequently, instead of feeling better, I felt worse. I felt violated, drew biased conclusions about myself, and began to think I needed to run away again.

Unfortunately, Aurora was the first to be targeted by my new discomfort. I apparently "bitched her out" on the phone because I didn't feel she was listening to or supporting me in the way that I needed, when I needed it. I demanded support and enthusiasm from her about my work, which was the only thing I could honestly share. In a fit of anger, I then took Melissa with me to her apartment to retrieve my items once again, although all she had of mine was a hat. I would call her again to patch things up—we would play a game of backgammon over cappuccino and hash—but for the most part my friendship with her had ended even before this outburst. Years later, I would briefly see her in Denver.

Luckily, it was a busy time of the year for the fashion industry and turned out to be a busy one for me as well. I had arrived in Milan at the wrong time during my first stay—right after the regular season was ending and before the shows. But when I returned after Tokyo, my timing was right on. Additionally, I had an excellent agency and numerous castings, and clients who may have remembered me from my earlier visits. (Hobbes was right to send me on so many go-sees when it was otherwise slow). One of these included a callback and an option to work for the illustrious magazine *Uomo Bazaar* (the Italian men's version of the international fashion mainstay). Another was for *L'uomo Vogue*, which was the Italian men's *Vogue* and the crème de la crème of all men's fashion magazines and counterpart to the incomparable *Women's Vogue*—considered the most influential fashion magazine of all time. Conde Naste Publications, who also owned *GQ*, owned *Vogue*. I considered *GQ* to be the most tantalizing men's fashion magazine in the world. It was in *GQ* that I first saw male models I fell in love with and wanted to emulate. After my callback for *L'uomo Vogue*, I got the job that would land me in American *GQ* for an Enrico Coveri ad in February and March (1994).

I arrived at the job at the justly named Super Studio in good condition, not hung-over or potted out. Three other models were there, all of whom had booked shows, big jobs, or were to become top male models—one later became the cover boy for Versace. The photographer was no less than Oliviero Toscani. The then-famous campaign of "The International Colors of Benetton" (which was a forerunner in the trend to showcase multi-ethnic faces in universal oneness) had been his brainchild.

During the shoot Maestro Oliviero sat on a stool in the middle of the studio. His assistants carried out every whim, from positioning the lighting to rewinding his film. A bevy of stylists and makeup artists were available on command and were exceedingly professional. Toscani's two children were there also as models. I had the great honor to stand in the center of the photo with other male models stretched out to my sides like a flock of geese. The two children looked nonplused and hugged one other model's and my leg. If I were astute I would have noticed that I was positioned again as a father figure. We male models were told to smile. After having had such a great experience smiling with the Stefanel campaign (which may have gotten me this job), I was not only in practice, but exceedingly confident, and it showed.

Perfectly dressed and detailed, positioned and lit, I looked directly ahead into the bulbous glass aperture of the camera that saw me with the eyes of millions. The camera clicked and flashed. "Smile larger," said Oliviero, and I did. "Not so large…Perfect," he said, and I responded. The large aperture lens repeatedly clicked. The light propelled itself around my contours like a blanket in the well-illuminated, white room. Suddenly all stopped. Before I knew it, it was all over.

FatherChristmas OnATear 13

The Holidays were fast approaching, and with them my usual melodramatic, seasonal despair. The day before Thanksgiving I lay on Cameron and Melissa's bed feeling friendless, depressed, and rejected by the world. Hewlett-Packard, and the United States, it seemed in retrospect, had rejected *me*. Tokyo had recently sent a fax stating that they felt it best I not come back—Milan was my best market, they kindly mentioned. Worse yet, I had asked Beatrice for money from my recent work and was flatly denied. I was told that I wouldn't get paid until they did, which may not be for a couple months.

When Cameron came home, I shared my money woes. The fact that Beatrice chose not to pay me enraged him. Instead of my taking his anger as support for me, I thought he was blaming me, which made me angry. I reacted strongly and then felt guilty. After he left, I turned to Melissa. The conversation quickly turned to sex. I told her of the two gay encounters I had already told Cameron about— Vova from Hamburg, and Fin, the first boy I had sex with in Chicago. Instead of truthfully telling her that I willingly accepted and enjoyed the experiences, I lied to her and myself and told her that Fin had "sexually molested me." The harshness of my condemnation may have motivated more honest comments afterwards in the privacy of my journal. Unfortunately, I also created another reason to obsess over money as if it held the solution I sought.

Journal, November 23: *I [told] Melissa about being victimized by Fin, but not telling her that I wasn't the victim when I sucked Vova's dick and also Rasmus's. I was the aggressor to a degree. I wanted more. I wanted to experience but-fucking him. I get horny to this day thinking of that. I was in love with Petey. I felt concerned about my homosexuality in high school when I wanted to go to the library and check out books concerning it but was afraid I might get caught doing it.*

I also felt that I was in love with Scott in Japan and [my best guy-friends] in college and graduate school. I felt sexually stimulated and wanted to fuck them. I really never was turned on by the women without serious contemplation and self imagery. The thought has just dawned on me after reading "The Road Less Traveled" that maybe I've never truly received love was because I never gave it. I want to be a model because I want to be famous. I want to have quick money and I want to prove to everyone that I can be successful at something. Fuck the car. Fuck the condo. Fuck San Diego for now. I'm going to stay here for Christmas.

Thanksgiving Day I sat around the apartment feeling like a trapped teenager. I turned to my journals, again telling myself that God and Jesus were there for me, much as I had turned to Jesus in my post-pubescent years. I felt as if "my energy was being depleted" and "my sensibilities, instincts, intelligence, and desires were being judged as wrong or stupid," despite no one but myself condemning me. I worried about whether Cameron would be "buzzed when he came home" and what his mood would be, much as I obsessed about my father's disposition as a youth. When he returned and was slightly drunk as I feared, an ensuing discussion took on distinct undertones to one I had with my father years before. Both resulted in my feeling belittled.

That evening, I left the apartment to attend a dinner party the agency was hosting in honor of the U.S. Thanksgiving Holiday. The restaurant was called *La Dolce Vita*, which couldn't have been more appropriate for the behavior that followed. Beatrice, the namesake of the agency and a grand dame diva, was there. So too were all the models, both male and female. I had anticipated that everyone would be on their best behavior given the stature of the restaurant and the presence of Beatrice, whom I thought of as a proper matronly woman. I couldn't have been more mistaken. The models acted like animals and the bookers cheered them on. Young female models in their late teens and early twenties drank cocktails by the fistful and squirmed on top of the boys and the table. The guys guffawed loudly at their simplistic and ridiculous conversation as some ate with their fists. I was amazed

144

that no one swung from the chandeliers. Yet it all seemed perfectly normal to everyone, including the other restaurant patrons, who must have been entertained by fiascos coordinated by modeling agencies and their tasteless mannequins. Would there ever be any sanity, anywhere, or any time in my life, I wondered.

One young woman, Ann, seemed to maintain the elegance and demeanor that appealed to me. She had all the traits I noted in my journal that I wanted in a woman—elegance, grace, and she was Belgian, which was close to being French. After the dinner Ann and I continued on to another bar and ended the night walking in the misty streets of Milan. Despite the perfection of what I started to think of as a romantic night, I had disturbing dreams of "taking trains guided by a homosexual who wanted me," and meeting "indifferent girls who wanted to get me high."

So much gay sex talk at home made me feel exposed. And money was tight. Therefore, that day I created the scenario that would result in my abandoning Cameron and Melissa before they could abandon me, and, once again, let me run away from my self-loathing. I took out half the money I had available to me, returned home, and informed Cameron that I had too little money to continue to live with them. He ignored me, which conveniently sparked the worst unresolved resentment I held for my dad. Angrily I told him I was leaving. Cameron was justifiably upset, which resulted in the ending of our friendship. The man whose photos helped launch my European trip of self-discovery had learned too much.

After paying my share of the phone bill, I took a cab to the Giusti, where I determined I had to live as a last resort. On the way to moving in with a roommate I remember little of, I bought my new household necessities—bananas, milk, yogurt, coke, a large quantity of hash, and a necklace with a cross on it. I stopped by a video casting that was predominantly focused on the body, but feeling distraught and self-conscious, left before going through with it. "Feeling dirty, hungry, hung-over, stressed-out, tired and hi," complete with "messy hair, pimpled face and shaved-off beard," I later went over to my new friend Ann's whose name is the same as my mother's. As with other pretty women, I misinterpreted our relationship. I misconstrued that first night to be a date. As the evening progressed I obsessed over when or how to kiss her, and then chastised myself incessantly for missing my opportunity.

Ann loved her hash joints and smoked them consistently—only Gregor rivaled her—and she easily surpassed Aurora's skill at rolling them—using two pieces of rolling paper instead of one to make jumbo joints, and torn-out fragments of her comp card she rolled into a tube and used as an elaborate filter. That night, she patiently instructed me on how to roll one. My hands trembled, causing me to flub up my lesson. Sheepishly, I gave the mess of paper, tobacco, hash, and filter back while asking if I'd get another chance. Her response was that I had my chance, which I thought meant that she would no longer take me as a lover—"I fucked up another one," I later wrote.

I remember little of my butch-acting, French roommate that ill-fated week in the Giusti, but religiously noted the mindless partying and many strangers during a time which was in many ways a regressed repeat of the former—it had lost the naive, playful charm I equated with my college days. I spent some of my time working out in my writings how I should think and what I should do in regard to my non-existent sexual relationship with Ann and what God and Jesus' expectations might be for me. My emotions lurched between positive self-affirmations and near suicidal misery.

I called my mother, most likely to cancel Christmas, and told her about the work and success—my Enrico Coveri, Baldessarini, *GQ*, and *Men's Journal* jobs—which I so strongly needed to believe in as a justification to her of my continued existence there. I spent the evening alone smoking dope and listening to "Believe in Yourself," by Lenny Kravitz, endlessly. Convincing myself that I take the song to heart, one early morning I layered myself in sweaters and climbed on the roof of the Giusti where I gave thanks that it was Christmastime and I was back where I had started—"the Alpha and the Omega," I wrote. Ann and I then spent a lovely day walking in the park past the carousel and donkey rides and watching what I described as "families bristling and lovers loving," before I went home to finish *The Road Less Traveled* and write poetry. By the end of the week, again on the roof of the Giusti, smoking hash alone, I contemplated my next move. My roommate was leaving for Paris, which meant that my rent would soon double. I would be left alone once again searching for a roommate in the now rather model-free industrial capital of Italy.

Luckily, Ann knew of a decent male model who had a place near her and was willing to take on a good guy. Sparky was from San Francisco. I thought he was a bit goofy-looking, and was never sexually attracted to him. He worked a lot of good-paying catalogs with Beatrice and his German agency, which meant he traveled a lot. He was neither a big drinker nor a big pot smoker—he once also commented, as Rudi had, that he never smoked more hash in his life than living with me. He had a great body from working out in the nearby gym, which I joined to work out with him. He worked regularly and had a reasonable amount of money he used for a modest but comfortable life style. All of this made him seem okay—at first.

Living with Sparky brought me back to the kind of semi-stability Gregor taught me was not only possible but also preferable as a professional model. I woke up at noon my first day as Sparky's new roommate, smoked a joint with him, and then let him take me food shopping. It would become part of my re-introduction to eating regular, healthy meals for the first time in many months. We had a wonderful lunch together which included a good, old-fashioned, American hamburger. Later that evening we went out to a club with five girls from Milan who were friends of his. One was a thick-boned, butch-acting, but delightful communist who took me to a workers' cafeteria to eat potatoes one day. The other was a petite, endearing, philosophy major who had a boyfriend and therefore relieved my anxiety that

147

I needed to find her sexually attractive. They eventually took me to museums, galleries, and on two trips to Florence, and provided me with all the cultural knowledge I had otherwise completely missed my entire time in their city.

The next day, although a Sunday, Sparky got up early and left for work. I reveled in an ideal pothead existence, which included sleeping until noon and then "waking and baking" by walking to Ann's apartment next door and smoking a giant joint with her (or, most likely, several). For the rest of that day, I never left the two buildings, moving back and forth between them, and smoking with Ann, doing laundry in her washing machine, and then eating a good meal that Sparky prepared. Returning to Ann's afterwards, I found myself sitting on her countertop in the kitchen as she cooked herself dinner. Confused about what our compatibility meant, I mustered up the courage to bend over and spontaneously kiss her on the cheek and then her ear. She didn't move. Afterwards she told me "she somewhat expected this." I felt cheap.

Nonetheless, having a pretty model girl imply that I was "normal" was everything I still could have imagined wanting to hear. I doubled my efforts at being straight. I started by giving Ann all of the clothing that made me feel effeminate, which included the red pants I had bought in Paris when I first arrived, a silk shirt that Lothar gifted and photographed me in, and a blue silk blazer my mother had bought me.

Confirmation of my immersion back into the illusion I was trying to create was the publication of my ad as Father Christmas to all of Italy. Having bought several magazines that contained the advertisement, I noticed that the copy read, "Live the Fantasy." I later wrote my reaction in my journal: "...I am Father Christmas on a tear... playing with being who I think I am...I am the maker of my own choices in life." I asked my journal if I would even be comfortable naked with Ann. Tellingly, I followed with the question "... or do I see her too much like a person like me?" This clearly defined the level of my disassociation between a same-sex partner and me. Was sex (with a man) so based in shame that I didn't yet think he could be a person like me?

Journal December 13: *I begin to feel uncomfortable, to look forward to and desire the attention and conversation from someone even more safe or forbidden, a male friend, comrad, buddy. I'm intrigued by whats behind my roommates psyche in a helpful and accepting way. Lets be honest, I do get more or less turned on by close touchy contact with a warm body, any warm body next to me, on a train, bus, subway, looking at maps, sharing intimate conversations. That's normal until one starts sporting a hard-on say in a conversation. The conversations with Sparky being alluded to are very often of a sexual nature (i.e. reading about circumcision in a Details magazine) crankin the shank to Magazines. I wonder if he isn't playing with me to – calling me home. In a way aren't I playing with them also?*

Ann and I continued spending time together. Sometimes she would date, return pensive or distraught, and tell me about it. One night after eating a turkey dinner Sparky had made for us, she confided in me that "the black hole was getting bigger inside her," and she saw herself "fighting against herself, never to be truly happy, even with everything given to her." My response was to "talk to her about religion." I told her "my god had no name," strategizing that I would hold off in telling her about Jesus until I sensed she was ready. She, in turn told me "her god was the moon."

The day after our religious talk, I left for Florence with my intellectual girlfriends. When I returned, Ann's mother was in town to celebrate her birthday and escort her home for the holidays. The show season for men would be starting right after the New Year, which kept her and most of the women out of town in early January. Sparky had returned from Switzerland, worked a job, wished Ann a stoney *bon voyage* before she left, and then left for the holidays as well. The girls I had recently gone to Florence with were spending time with their parents, and even the drug dealer was on vacation—all leaving me in the horrific situation of being without hash or connections to get hash.

149

In addition to this, I felt I was coming down with a cold. I decided to take advantage of this reprieve from the abuse my body had been taking, make the best of it, and give everything up, including smoking and sugar. Luckily I had borrowed several books from the Italian girls—Oscar Wild's *Dorian Gray* and *The History of Milan in Detail*, which was a professional tour operator's guide to the city. Starting on Christmas Day and for the six days that followed I fended off my detoxifying body by spending hours walking throughout the entire city, following the book's indices of where Milan's ancient Roman and Medieval walls stood, and viewing the ancient ruins and architectural wonders standing within them.

On Christmas Day, after a long walk by many churches and baroque mansions that necessitated I pee on a eighteenth century, neoclassic temple, I attended a Catholic Christmas communion, which I wasn't supposed to participate in since I wasn't Catholic and had never confessed. I wrote "…It's funny that just when I am restling with the tugs of Catholicism as a spiritual outlet, if not something I might go along with because of its availability and similarity to Christianity, I read *The Road Less Traveled*, which nullifies any leisure for me to get caught up in superficial ritual." Later, feeling lonely and abandoned, I wrote, "I feel far from anyone I called friend or brother but am now indifferent to and far from anyone I called lover but no longer long for I am weary of life, can't sleep, and fear death."

The following day I went to six churches and prayed in many. Seeing an old woman weeping in one, I smiled, she smiled back at me, and I noted, "she would inherit the kingdom, I'm sure." I positioned myself right under a light to feel as if the light of heaven were on my head, I suppose. I prayed for success and later took the shoes I had bought in Munich and threw them in the trash, which truly would come to symbolize that my prayer was answered, even if the later success that I had asked for ended up looking far different than I may have supposed.

Two days after Christmas, I stopped in seven churches and

prayed in them all. Once back to my apartment I determined "I am responsible for heaven's rejoicing" and decided "to give up homosexual anything as I did with cigarettes and alcohol." The following day, "I had sex with myself while thinking about my first sexual experience with my first girl friend." I "felt healed giving to the good vagina." But I also acknowledged that I did what I always did, which was "to force myself to think about having sex with a woman just before I came so that I could consider my visualization as being heterosexual and train myself to like it."

After masturbating to thoughts of heterosexuality, I became paranoid about Sparky. I measured the dimensions of the room—it was 18'×12'—and realized for the first time that I had been living in a small space. When he returned I lay awake in bed "freaking out about our energies" and thinking again that I should "become a minister." An extremely hash-filled New Year's Eve in Florence followed (to make up for the suffering I endured by having given up my vices) with the Italian girlfriends. And as soon as the agency re-opened, I immediately complained to my bookers about my apartment. There seemed to be no replacement for the repeated behavior of potentially sabotaging my progress by complaining about my living quarters to my booker just before a busy season. The booker simply said, "This is a business," and left it at that.

My next activity upon the resumption of life and business as normal was to have the San Diego credit union I banked at repossess my car. My acquaintance hadn't made a single payment and lied to them (after I tried to handle the situation by giving the credit union her number from Tokyo) that she was out of town for months. I contacted her mother, found out where her daughter worked, contacted the credit union, and had the jeep voluntarily repossessed.

The show season momentum began immediately thereafter. Male models moved to Milan from all over the world and my former quiet Milan exploded into frenzied insanity. Castings for designers and major international agencies increased to five or six per day.

151

Male models had to stand in endless, long lines of upwards of 2,000 models. Waiting in these lines was tedious, competitive, and nerve racking. Everyone checked each other out and conversations ran from the mundane—cute chicks and working out—to the catty—whose book was better. Groups of men stood around looking cool, smoking cigarettes like so many James Deans. So soon after supposedly quitting smoking, I started buying full packs on a regular basis.

Inversely proportional to male modeling becoming more popular and seemingly glamorous, the number of men used per show and the payments made to them decreased. Added to this was uncertainty of where fashion was going—it was rumored to be dead, but it actually was dramatically changing. Some designers used classic, heterogeneous, attractive models, while others increasingly utilized multi-cultural men, breaking the mold of the basic good-looking, white European guy who had earlier represented the style I had been positioning myself for. An exotic, American Hispanic man moved from Paris to stay with Sparky and I. His Dolce & Gabbana photos made him look like Satan. He carried himself and acted with an unaffected nonchalance that worried me. Not only did I find him somewhat eerie—which was what I felt the entire fall collections to be—but his mannerisms gave away that he was gay—and gay with no inhibition against saying anything that was on his mind. He gave me very little wiggle-room in my constant dire need to prove my heterosexuality. Nonetheless, his cutting-edge, unique look *was* in, and he knew it. Soon we learned he had more shows than anyone else in the city: Versace, Armani, Krizia, Trussardi, Dolce & Gabbana, Inghirami, Ferre, and Valentino.

Events moved at a breathtaking pace. Friday the 7th of January, castings included Marzotto, followed by Krizia, then Fujiwara, the French Agency PH1, Verri, and Studio Garibaldi for Katharine Hamnett. The line for Verri was one of the worst. It wrapped around an entire city block and up the staircase of a modern office building to a small studio. At the end was a tiny room painted white with elaborate gold molding and all walls lined with mirrors. At one end sat several men at an ornate, white desk that was equally embellished with gold. The men took several seconds to look at each model's book while the model was instructed walk quickly back and forth. At first I thought there was no way on earth I could possibly stomach the inane behavior of the male models or the length of the line. To my great delight I persevered. I later discovered they contracted me for the show.

By Sunday, I learned that I had also gotten the Fendi show, which I worked the following day (Monday). The show was a standing show. The models (all male) were positioned on podiums around a small room. Photographers, buyers, editors, and the international fashion elite walked by, took photos and notes, and sometimes felt the fabric of the exquisite, classically tailored clothes that fit me like none other. I sat on a chair playacting that I was a Russian aristocrat, worthy of the beautiful clothes that my stature was selling. I was grateful to have brought my Tolstoy, *Master and Man,* which helped me get into my role. The projection worked, and I would later find a rare photo of me in a show catalogue.

I must have done a good job since the following day (Tuesday). I was summoned to a fitting for the Fusco show (Fusco being upper-end Fendi). Even the fitting room was opulent. I was given magnificent, plush cashmere coats and kid leather gloves to try on. I stood alone on a square stage roped off by opulent cording that made it look like a one-person boxing ring.

After the fitting, I rushed to the Verri show. Male models were styled in retro-punk hairdos and placed on stages beneath an elaborate metal contraption. Modern, synthesized techno music played as viewers walked around a floor covered in sand. Bright colored and white lights were attached to metal beams to the sides and above us. Models moved within their stations to center themselves better in moveable white diffused lanterns. Some adjusted them to improve the photos being taken by roaming photographers. Having only taken direction in the past without much emphasis on paying attention to what was really happening, I did not know anything of working with lighting. Neither the absent producers of the show, nor the photographers, gave me any direction. I felt my performance was lackluster and wardrobe ridiculous and was grateful to never see a photo from this show.

The Fusco show Wednesday morning was once again a standing show. The clothing was exquisite, but our performance was dull, requiring only that we all stand like immobile mannequins in a window with no props. Immediately after, I rushed over to the agency where I was to see Elite from Paris. This would prove enlightening.

That evening I visited my old friend Lothar, who was also in town and, as usual, at the Giusti. We smoked hash and drank hard liquor, and then sat alone in his room as he had me stare into his eyes while he performed "staring hypnosis" on me as he did my first weekend in Milan (to supposedly help me break through my secrets and gain his and my own trust). It must not have worked, for I didn't record saying anything profound about myself, except for disclosing my belief in Jesus Christ. The next day we went out to Hollywoods, like the old days—Lothar knew the PR guys and got us a VIP table. But it was no longer the old times. Later I recorded I was disgusted with having danced the night away with transsexuals. Although I would supposedly see him and Zoë again in Paris, I don't remember anything about this.

The following day, amidst the flotsam of the show castings, I got a call from the agency. Elite Model Management, the Parisian agency, wanted to represent me for the Paris shows and to be my agent. I would need to move to Paris in two days. My dream had come true—I was finally accepted by a Paris agency. I had achieved what I wanted when I first flew from San Diego, a chance to make it in the most prestigious fashion city in the world. Paris would soon come to symbolize the end of my old illusions and the beginning of the reality I secretly had been avoiding, but knew to be the real reason for my trip.

I immediately called Luuk in Belgium, whom I had been keeping in touch with, and then began to pack. I went to the roof of the ancient Duomo and looked over Milan. It hadn't changed during the past months. Had I? To end on a good note, I gave money and a candle to a lady at a church and more to a man with a dog on the sidewalk. I bought chestnuts, which were being roasted on an open fire, had a suntan, and went to an artist exhibition with my Italian girlfriends who I promised to—and did—keep in touch with for awhile. At some point "I stepped in dog shit for the first time," and noted it meant "I had seen everything in Milan, and it is time to go." The following morning I stopped by the agency to say bye to my bookers, and confirmed my arrival in Paris with Eve, who gladly invited me back. The subway and train were all on time that day, I noted, as I left the city for the last time.

What I Really Want Is Love 14

S how castings lasted for the entire week and through the weekend. Elite sent me to Christian Dior, Sonya Rykiel, Kenzo, Gaultier, Issey Miyake, Montana, and a show publicity agency called Totem that would be transformative. I wasn't hired for any of them and ended the show season with "horrible diarrhea," which I thought was either "Parisian stomach flu from Metro hands, or my superstitions."

It was immediately discernable that the agency was more concerned with its highly profitable Women's Division. The Men's Division, even if it *was* Elite Hommes International, was lucky to be in existence. This two-tiered structure was obvious in the agency's layout. Men had an alternative, less obvious entrance, were not to interact with the women, and had a secondary booking area, where, unlike in Milan, male models were not allowed to loiter—unless you were a very high-level model. There *were* exceptions to every rule in Paris.

The bookers' personalities were stereotypical of the setting. The female head booker was an extremely well dressed, elegant woman from whom gaining any acknowledgement whatsoever seemed an excruciatingly tiresome task. One of her subordinates was an openly gay man who seemed one of the most well-adjusted and normal people I met. A second subordinate was a young woman who was obviously taking after her mentor, uncommunicative and completely uninformative.

I lived in Paris for a month during which time the weather was rainy, chilly and thereby unfavorable to my adopted Southern California sensibilities. Many of my Milan roommates, acquaintances, and friends were in town: Gregor, Sparky and his friend Marco, Rusty, my friend who I met for Brunch on the "Christian Holiday," and

Simone. Despite this I felt lonely. The modeling community that made Paris its home resided and socialized in close-knit circles instead of the collegiate dorm-like settings in Milan and Tokyo. And Paris' reputation as the world capital of elegance and sophistication daunted me.

Living with my graduate school acquaintance Eve, I realized how detached I was, which made me feel isolated. It wasn't until my second week in Paris, during the slow time, when I didn't have to feel like I was having sex under stress, that I mustered the ability to fuck her—"with a rubber so that I could reserve my true being," I wrote. Before, during, and after, I chastised myself for being a prostitute for a free place to live. "Eve had short hair," and, of all things, "didn't talk enough," amid other reasons I devised for disliking her. But I noted that I was working on making myself famous. I no longer saw a conflict with success and my Christianity ("if others could do it with whatever on their side, I sure could as a Christian," I reasoned), and felt it was nice that "I had power over women (to attract them, draw out their vanity and make them dream," I wrote), even though, "getting older, I had less power over homosexual men." I wondered "how much power even God had in the modeling industry—it seemed more run by luck than anything else," I wrote. "Why else would I have given all my power to Jesus yet still have such an abysmal money situation?"

I confessed to myself that I didn't take modeling seriously when I was in Tokyo because I felt protected by the contract. I had heard that in Paris the agency would pay for your apartment and food, but I was now educated to the fact that it required that I work to pay it back. It was maddening that despite my prior show successes within ten days of living in Paris, I was down to my last $33. To cover, I took a cash advance and maxed out my credit card. I called my mom, in utter humiliation, to beg her to send a wire transfer to me, and visited the embassy to determine when a potential tax refund from my comparatively lucrative HP days could be obtained.

I acknowledged that smoking dope, which I now found from honest and dishonest Rastafarians in the Paris Metro, was "dangerous

(I got ripped off again), costly, a crutch, and made me lose focus."I decided that stress from cigarettes, caffeine, alcohol, drugs, money worries, concerns over where to live, eat, and how to pay rent, boredom in modeling lines, and tedious daily traipsing to the grocery store, caused acne. Acne, in turn caused more worry and my inability to do my best work. I compared my acne to Job of the Bible: "Job lost everything in the desert, his home and family, and was covered with boils, but persisted in his love for God." Likewise, I believed that God existed because when I had tried to deny Him, I felt instead "an almost disturbing ray of inner joy and peace." Since God existed, "my only problem with acne must be my vanity—but I was not a Dorian Gray." I eventually sought dermatological treatment but complained I couldn't maintain it because of lack of money, which made the whole dilemma come full circle again.

I looked for apartments where I could live without the fear of having to have sex with Eve, while going to a very small number of castings, which were mostly for other agencies. Storm, one of the best agencies in London, decided to take me, but I knew I couldn't afford to move and live there. The German agencies that paid well still didn't find me lucrative—I wasn't very commercial, so I was told. My friendly, gay Parisian booker told me that I should stay, work on my book with tests, and travel to make money. I listened and immediately scheduled two tests.

The first was with a photographer named Felix, who shot me on a rainy day in his Parisian apartment. The apartment was set up just for this purpose. One corner contained professional lighting on a back wall and floor composed of reflective material one would find in a studio. I had had no access to cool wardrobes and wasn't very creative in thinking about how to borrow any. We managed to dig around his closet and find some worn and baggy linen suit jackets, shirts, and cotton sweater-like shirts, white socks and sweats. The wardrobe, combined with my long, shaggy, and styled-to-look-messed-up hair made me look like a homeless person wearing the remnants of the

158

wardrobe from the movie *Fame*.

Prior to, during, and after the shoot, Felix produced a good quantity of hash, which, against my better judgment, I smoked with reckless abandon. Despite the resulting self-consciousness, I felt a comforting familiarity. His dog Dozer sat nearby, while we smoked and talked, which reminded me of pleasant memories of a former best friend (Petey's brother) who likewise sat with his dog while we got stoned and talked about everything. This time, I supposedly learned all about my direction, focus, realistic expectations about life in Paris, strategy, and financial aspects of the business, though I remember nothing of this. I also, quite profoundly, indicated in my writings that I had realized a great spiritual truth: "what I am really in Paris for is simply *the experience*." If I had taken this to heart, it may have reduced the nearly unbearable angst I constantly felt about love, money and career.

The second test was with a female photographer, named Celeste, who was beautiful, intelligent, and an outstanding photographer. As one of a few successful female photographers, she later confided in me how difficult it was for women to break into the industry. Despite wearing clothes that she had borrowed, which were, as usual, too long for me, the shoot was one of the best I had. I felt comfortable, confident and at ease. She captured me without the need to use modeling tricks by building up my ego with flattery and telling me that a million men wanted to be me and do what I was doing. To add life and playfulness to our adventure, she made me pretend that we were shooting a movie and I was the young star. We shot all around the Les Halles area of Paris, which was where I lived. This further added to the familiarity that allowed me to feel I was at home with my work.

We hung out that evening for the first of many times in what became our favorite pub—The Frog and Rosbiff. There she told me what I recorded as "the most horrifying story of a woman called Calypso and a haunted Gestapo house where models lived; and how this woman is wicked and gets her kicks out of fucking with people and destroying

159

boys' careers if she doesn't like them or if they don't fuck her." I later described how the story made me "feel like a prostitute," displayed how "sexual fucking around leads to personal destruction," and "made bad karma." Our continued friendship was easily maintained since it was non-sexual and therefore non-threatening. I believed she liked me for me, and that she believed in me and my potential.

One evening after drinking three pints of Guinness, I disclosed that I had already drunk a bottle of wine before meeting her and still didn't feel drunk. After a long talk over yet more drinks, I left confused, thinking that perhaps "I was becoming too much like Jim Morrison— who died a pitiful alcoholic in Paris" and whose grave I had visited three years earlier. Nonetheless, until the time I left Paris, we spent nearly every night drinking together in the pub.

By my third week in Paris, having had no work and broke once again, I was told on a Wednesday that by Friday a decision would be made as to whether or not I could stay, or as in Tokyo and Milan, be asked to leave. This time, I didn't care. My love affair with Paris was over for the time being, and I was "feverish, tired and in a very bad way." I decided "what I really want is love." To get it, I decided, "I must show it." Acting on this, I took empathy on my bookers and brought them a gift of chocolates. The next day instead of being fired, I learned that I had a job to work for *French Cosmopolitan*. It wouldn't be an editorial or promotional job, but a section on philosophy, which needed photos to accompany an article of how couples moved apart in a relationship. The job seemed a metaphor for what my experiences with all of my girlfriends had been.

I wore two outfits—one sunny and bright and another dull and gray. I was told to be affectionate with the blond, pseudo-wife in the first shot, and bored and distant in the second. I got the second down but had trouble with the first. The girl did little, I thought, to encourage a romantic display. I, in turn, felt nothing towards her. Had I accepted that I was gay, I would have at least been able to pretend that I was straight. Instead, I self-consciously floundered in self-judgment and failed attempts at convincing seduction. The result was a photo that looked like I was biting her leg.

Two days after, I told Eve I was looking for an apartment, and exactly one month after I had again arrived in Paris, Elite got a call from the Spanish agency Jet Set. I had first seen Jet Set at the end of the show castings of my first week. I had then been asked to make a photocopy of my book, which Elite submitted to Jet Set, most likely for review and to "suss out" my potential. Now Jet Set was willing to represent me and wanted me the next morning. I had a job for that coming Monday. They even purchased my plane ticket, which they put on account. In the spirit of friendship, Eve treated me to an exquisite last night's dinner. Early the next morning I left for Madrid for what I thought would be "two weeks of exercise, nutrition, healing and work."

Tynnker And I Are Bisexuals 15

I arrived in Spain with the best intentions and, as ever, with no money. I took a taxi from the airport to a meeting point where a Scottish man named Bill met me. Bill spoke with such a thick Scottish accent that I asked what language he was speaking. He nonetheless got me to where I was going, which was a hostel where I would stay, and which the agency had agreed to pay for on account. Over all, the residence was quite pleasant. I had a small room with a tiny sink, and the toilet was just down the hall. My French windows, hung with lacey drapes, had pretty, wooden blinds and opened to a narrow, green, wrought iron balcony on which sat potted succulents similar to those I was familiar with in Southern California. The climate was much more like California as well, which was a nice welcome from the rainy, chilly Paris I had just come from.

My room looked across to another stone building built around the same time—most likely the early twentieth century. Similar buildings made up the block. The area was close to the center of the city, so during my stay there I was able to walk and then later rollerblade everywhere. On one occasion, the street directly in front of my house filled with marchers carrying a red banner. I quickly discovered that the restlessness of the Spanish people didn't only manifest itself in marches. Newly liberated from decades of fascist repression, the Spanish people were hungry for freedom to express themselves, which resulted in a burgeoning social scene unlike anything anywhere else in the world. To my dismay, I learned that teenagers, young adults, mothers, fathers, grandparents, families with children, and everyone in-between went out to dinner after ten p.m. and then walked around the streets at night, going to pubs, or just hanging out until 4 a.m., with many not retiring until sunrise. My room, like the rest of the hostel, was on the second floor, which was directly above the cacophony. By my second night, Saturday, and the middle of a typical rambunctious weekend, I had written in my Franklin "the room is so horribly noisy at all hours of the night, I'm beginning to hate Spain…this is another Hell." Once again I was at odds with what I wanted for myself—"peace of mind and hope for sobriety"—and the reality that I found myself in—conflict and war with my ever-persuasive addictions.

My feelings for Spain would soon change as I realized what a wonderful place it was. Not only was the weather mild, but the people were pleasant, easy-going, non-judgmental, and otherwise unpretentious. That was, all except for my landlady. Belinda was a relatively strict Catholic, with two grown children and a deceased husband. Her daughter, who also worked as the maid and often cooked the family's meals, was ever-present and affable. Her late-teenaged son, who kept a close eye on me and the other roomers, behaved properly only when his mother was around, and otherwise acted out whenever he could. The family's rooms were also on the same floor, which was a long rectangle with roomers all along the outside minus one space where the Senorita had a television. The television was strictly off limits for roomers, but one could find Senorita Belinda sitting in her comfortable chair, watching the bullfights and often enjoying a large, steaming cup of espresso with thick milk on weekend afternoons. The family's kitchen was directly across from my room and off limits to me and the other lodgers. Starting in the early morning well before I got up, I began to hear the sounds of food preparations and the gurgle of the Italian espresso maker taunting me. I didn't even have a refrigerator. Every evening when I was home, I also heard dishes clinking and smelled well-cooked meals flowing in from beneath my door.

Although I worked relatively often, the pesetas I earned amounted to very little and were not easily forthcoming from the agency. The agency fee, although lower than Milan, Paris, or Tokyo was still a substantial 35%, and to my immediate displeasure, payment wouldn't be made until three months after a job—if that. Within a couple of days I was down to $5, and then $1, at which time, after claiming like Scarlet O'Hara "I will never go hungry again," I demanded and received miniscule cash advances from the agency. My food consisted of fruits and vegetables I bought at the farmers' market. Feeling impoverished, "I saved the rubber band of a stalk of carrots" and dramatically wrote "I understand the minds of bag people." My staple meal, which I loved, became an open-face sandwich with canned tuna, chopped onion and tomatoes, using the tuna oil as a dressing, and a banana, all of which I kept on my window ledge at night to keep cool.

Much as in Paris, I didn't live with other models in Spain, which required I make an effort to socialize with them. Living in a hostel meant that I also interacted with other city dwellers and native Spaniards. I was, however, the only American model at my agency, which contributed to my feeling special. But I worried that this agency was substandard compared to the other elite agencies that represented me, especially since it also ran a modeling school to make ends meet. Frequently impoverished and removed from my peers, I spent a lot of time in my little room writing and reading. My first book, which I began that first night, was *Dune*. I would also read *Les Miserables, The Odyssey, Candide, The Wordsworth Handbook of Kings & Queens,* Machiavelli's *The Prince,* and three of Hemingway's books, which were often written about Spain and bullfights. I hated the thought of bullfights but decided that I would be open-minded about them, and maybe even go to one if I had the chance. This never materialized.

Because of the wonderful climate, another amusement included working out in the park. One of my favorite parks, El Retiro, had stations where one could stop one's jog and do pull-ups on pig bars and push-ups or sit-ups in designated grassy areas. In addition to its wonderful parks, Spain also boasted an enormous open-air flea market every Sunday called the Rastro, which took place in central Madrid, not too far from where I lived, and hosted thousands of stalls, interesting people, and street performers. My first noted interaction there was with an Arab to whom, in the course of negotiating the cost of incense, I complained bitterly about "living in such utter, fucking poverty." He told me "I was rich because I come with my fucking American dollars." Not dissuaded, I continued to tell him of my trials and tribulations: how I couldn't take it anymore; that I had to quit and get a real job; how I felt so utterly useless, so poor, and unable to choose even basic things like rest without noise, food when I wanted it, to pay for my laundry to be done, or to buy a new shirt at the Rastro.

He stopped my banter to ask what I was looking for. I told him I wanted travel experience and a nice girl. He then told me of a friend of his that, like me, had "bummed around the world like a hippy and now led 20,000 men in spirituality." My reply was that I felt an urge for spiritual leadership after reading the book *Dune*. He kindly replied that I had agreed long before to what I would do spiritually. I replied that I couldn't quit modeling now as a failure. He concluded the conversation by saying I should look for God in my travels, and when I found him, and my communication with him was developed, all the rest would come.

The rest of my walk, spanning two days and covering much of the city, was much less inspirational. My next stop was a pharmacy where I went to buy earplugs. There an "old queen" apparently asked me about prophylactics. The conversation escalated to his telling me to "stick my earplugs up my ass." I later wrote that ("respectful in my response, cool-headed and indifferent to him and his miserable attitude") I told him his prophylactics were a good idea and left. I then went to the park, past a statue that I described as "a somber woman holding an almost evil-looking, smiling mask above her head."

I ran into an English clown who was drinking a beer and smoking a cigarette with a red smile painted on his face and a broken happy meter on his hat. He apparently "gave out balloons to children and disgusting, perverted jokes to adults." He bought me a beer as I was going for coffee to gather enough energy to finish my walk. I asked for a cigarette. He said he'd buy anything for me. At first I conversed with him about "fucking rich people." As we continued to talk, we shared stories of how we were running away from home. We spoke of being on stage behind the mask, cheering people up, and playing the game. He said that he could take the mask off, and asked, "Could you?" I wrote in my journal that my response was "No." I walked home that day, stopping at the Ritz Carlton with a piece of bread in my pocket saved from lunch to have as my dinner. People noticed me there, thinking I had money, I noted, although I knew I had none. But I was ready for tomorrow, ready to sell clothes. That night I "prayed for guidance in communicating with God."

The week began with good news. One of the castings I went to that first day was a job for the next and I had an option for another—an advertisement for the very important Spanish version of *Cosmopolitan*. The job starting the next day and lasting for two, was for an entire editorial spread—a total of six pages for me and six pages for a sexy gorgeous male model also from San Diego—in the magazine insert of the newspaper *El Pais*. *El Pais* was Spain's largest newspaper, read by 6,000,000 people. The insert editorial would have me and the other model dressed in major designers ranging from Armani to Valentino and some major Spanish designers as well.

The first thing I did when I found out about the job was to call my grandmother, who I called "Omi," back in the States. Omi was always a realist, a German Russian born in St. Petersburg in 1906, whose primary purpose was constantly to inform my mother and me how we could strive always to do better. Consequently, we never could do or be enough. Enthusiastically I spoke into the phone (recording later in my journal every word of the conversation) that I had not only been in Spain for one working day but also already had a job. Omi immediately asked how much it paid. Despite recording every detail of my expenses and saving every single receipt, I had no idea. I nervously laughed and said I'd find out tomorrow, at which point she informed me how much she "didn't believe in this modeling stuff."

My excitement was immediately quashed, fueling the

continual diatribe I had with myself about my family not supporting me emotionally. Crushed at the poor timing of my grandmother's statement, I neglected to acknowledge that I had set myself up by calling her right before what I considered my debut and a future of assured health and prosperity. This incident resulted in my declaring, on paper at least, that I must believe in myself if not for my own sake, then for God—my agent Falco believed in me, as did others, and "somewhere, somehow, someone was applauding with me."

The next day truly was the job of my career, and one that tugged at every fiber of my body to come to terms with myself. The title of the photo spread, which was a story of two men, was *Sin Barriers*—No Barriers. Interestingly, that morning I had two gay dreams—one with Petey holding my hand and putting his head on my gut and another of not being allowed to join in the fun that a group of gay guys were having because I said I wasn't gay. The front cover of the magazine would contain an image of an asteroid plummeting into the Earth and the copy would read "The End of the World." What was eventually to come would truly be the end of the world as I saw it.

The shoots were sexually stimulating. I dressed in Armani pajamas and, later, an Armani business suit. An evening appearance had me standing in candlelight on a balcony, holding a drink. My modeling partner worked on his own spreads wearing a dashing red outfit in one, and sumptuous, sensual, colorful clothes and sweaters in others. He too had a sexy pose in the evening, which later appeared in the magazine across from my evening pose, hinting of a romantic night between the two of us. The enormous, twelve-page, magazine spread portrayed two handsome men going through their respective days, dressed appropriately for their complementary characters—his clothing representing a sexy, chipper, and more risqué personality and mine a more distant, moody temperament. The beautifully photographed images and resplendent settings would be works of art evoking the gay coupling that Spain would soon be a frontrunner in supporting.

That day I competitively judged the gorgeous San Diego model to be "an asshole." Nonetheless, I also acknowledged in my journals that I felt "turned on sexually." That evening as I ate an orange to stave off my hunger and listened to the sounds of the family across the hall gorging on their complete meal, I again wrote that the feeling the shoot gave me "felt like sex," which I interpreted to mean "being used and using." Nonetheless, the accumulation of that and the following day's work were important steps in my coming out. In the short term, the male model I worked with provided fuel for many masturbation sessions.

Journal February 23: *[We viewed the Polaroid's from the work from the day before and] I felt a dislike for myself…me the conservative, classic guy and that handsome body of a dude from San Diego who was more of the gigolo, more of the wild guy. Both of us so much in common. I felt as if it was more of a play on homosexuality. The two of us some sort of a couple. I'm sure the thought pushed through everyone's mind. It was clear as day—as ying and yang. I felt somehow stimulated by it, turned red when I asked him what he normally does on the weekend. He said he wouldn't be here maybe. Seemed nice and had the same sort of eye contact if not promoting it. We stood close enough together the photographer had to keep separating us. I felt some jealousy and admiration from him as well. I guess what drove me to two cigarettes today, a beer and lunch and major insecurity just after the shoot was this rustle with homosexuality in the scene and my own reactions of blushing and obvious childish adoration of a type. I told of my relationship with Eve—why? I felt so obvious and in giving this obviousness away, I felt ashamed. God knows I'm not interested nor would ever be in any sort of even friendship with this egotistical obnoxious guy, but I was embarrassed all the same and felt out of control and agitated. I think this most of all, this playing on the homo-editorial, like the playing on the business man yesterday which gave me a nightmare last night was the most disturbing as well as my financial horror situation, just before the shoot. It's acting, this acting thing even for still photography that I love. I can't let it phase me and just realize it for what it is. It's true, I have homoerotic parts of my past and in imagination that I can't let phase me. I know who I am and what I want. I must trust in faith and continue this growth in faith. I must know what I want and am for it. No homosexual experience or future even fits into that path*

168

and soberly I'm not interested. It's a part of all of us. Another stumbling block that these assholes try to put in ones way.

I spent the rest of that week exercising in El Retiro and did not drink or do drugs—my longest abstinence in nearly a year. The abstinence did not last long, however, and resulted in intense cravings for "a bar, a drink, and a cigarette" that I equated with all the fun the crowds were having on the noisy street below. Soon I engaged in finding the people and activities that would nurse my cravings and feed my resentments. Thus, a cycle repeated itself: forced abstinences erupted into terrible binges, which led back to renewed abstinences. Concurrent with this came equally dramatic cycles of sexual honesty and denial.

After my first big night on the bar scene that included elaborate, rocking discos and trendy pool bars named Hanoi, Arches, and Ole Madrid, I woke up with the pimples I had recovered from in Italy. I recognized this as "a warning against future dalliances." But interestingly my experiences also resulted in my first acknowledgement that I was even gayer than I had previously admitted. "My sexual mode's leaning towards the 50% 40% homo base now," I wrote. Unfortunately, thinking that I had a choice, I concluded with a comment that this direction I didn't want to feel or follow.

Journal March 5: *Those high school torturing grounds are over. The jocks have retired to weekend athletics. Terror of the football field is over. My biggest error was in not realizing how beautiful I was and that that turned some of the boys on just as much as the girls. It's always been my choice and yes I have always been fascinated by the male body (the frame, the muscles but not the genitals). The women's but and tits and pussy seem to me more of pristine beautify like a photograph or painting. But I am drawn to them. Sexually I've had no problems getting hard. Visually, though in fantasy its harder for me to picture or recall the most satisfying moments without a feeling of detachment. This feeling, especially after fucking a girl, is more like, now go away or move over. Or what have I now entangled myself with. Like so much baggage or material possessions even which become nothing more than a joyless responsibility.*

One week after my first job, I worked a *Cosmopolitan* advertisement in which I was portrayed as a surfer boyfriend. I shared about my "homosexual experiences" soon after with a new friend, Stella, who I enjoyed because she, like my Italian girlfriends, was not a model (she was in Spain teaching English as a second language). I followed my tales with my usual caveat about my lack of interest in having sex with men. She said it wasn't important what I had done, but what I intended to do in the future. Being the nice Jewish girl from Beverly Hills that she was, she followed her advice with a non-Christian viewpoint, as well. She kindly shared with me that I was to take responsibility for my actions, actively work on forgiving myself, and not dump my shit on God. This made a lot of sense to me and helped me along in my next pertinent step.

The next day, I befriended a new best friend named Tynnker. Tynnker was an extremely sexy woman who was supposedly a New York Mafioso's girlfriend—although she was from Texas. I met her at a casting, and as we took the Metro home, she disclosed to me that she had asked Jesus Christ that, if he got her on the cover of the Spanish *Cosmopolitan,* she would give up hash. She apparently got the Cosmo job and offered me the hash. I greedily accepted. We went to her apartment where I got stoned and we spent the next hours talking about sexuality. She told me that she was a bisexual, and I told her that I was one too—"Tynnker and I are both bisexual," I wrote in my journal. It was then, the first time since I knew I was in love with Petey, that I even suggested to anyone that I was anything but straight—in the past I had only admitted to gay actions but not being. In retrospect, I wished that I hadn't been stoned so that I could have dealt with it with a clear mind.

I realized it was still hard for me to accept, and I wanted what I considered heterosexual life to be—"sanity and cleanliness in a fucked up world." I asked Tynnker why, "why were we so?" She answered "it was because we were beautiful people and could attract other beautiful people." There was "no denying that there was some sort

170

of sexual turn on to that." This didn't completely sit right with me. Instead, I continually conjectured every possible excuse, and looked for every possible angle for why I couldn't accept being the gay part of the bisexual that I had just declared myself to be. "The beautiful-men thing was stimulating and normal—although most men supposedly developed natural defense mechanisms against them, such as macho sportsmanship, being a slut with other women, or competition," I wrote. "Beyond normal and stimulating was nothing and nowhere," I feared. What I needed was to find a woman who was "okay with my past and okay with my fantasies." Despite Tynnker not being perfect— "a beautiful working girl, apparently with good taste, though needy for friendship and love, loud, boisterous, vain and nouveau-riche to the Texas 'T'"—and most likely because she was unavailable, she became the target of my newest female obsession of the week.

After eating a meal together, early in the fast but dramatic friendship that followed, we returned to her apartment where I smoked hash, listened to her read from her journals, and did sit-ups on her floor in my boxer shorts. She was still not smoking dope in her effort to keep her promise with God for the cover. I, on the other hand, later confusingly wrote "I smoked because it turned off my sexual drive, increased the allure, and turned down my intellectual mind a few notches." Re-enacting the situations that most irked me with Aurora, I listened as she ranted and "played stupid about my own wisdom in order to make her feel more knowledgeable." But since we were both bisexual, we took our playacting even further. As I lay there that later afternoon, she exposed her bare ass and breasts-in-a-bra and had me touch them to either confirm their fake or natural firmness of which she was so proud. I went home and apparently "masturbated to thoughts of her body and lacy underwear covering her shaved pussy." But I couldn't help having "flash thoughts of the guy from San Diego" I had modeled with. I finally "got off to images of her saying 'Fuck me, Homosexual.'"

I later tried to convince myself that this was the first time, maybe ever, that a woman had turned me on so. I was supposedly frightened by her wealthy, Mafia boy friend's power and capacities, which I justified as a good reason for my not really being that interested in her. Of the boyfriend, I noted, "he wanted him for his money, respected him like a father, but wasn't sexually attracted." Why did she not act on the fact that I, on the other hand, "could provide so much more sexually, emotionally and spiritually? Perhaps, she had problems—she was rather distant and clearly in need of recovery from her pot and ecstasy addiction," I reasoned.

As our fast, furious, and insane friendship progressed past our initial courtship, we swung on swing sets during sunset in Retiro Park while we talked about grade school, dined together, and talked about the business, life, love, and the pursuit of dreams. On one occasion, Tynnker invited me to shave my entire body, which I did—the act turned me on by reminding me of the gay barber incident in Milan. She also suggested I learn to rollerblade. The following day, I bought a pair and took up a past time that allowed me to explore the parks and streets of Madrid as well as have countless hours of enjoyable exercise and sightseeing. On the side of the box of my new blades was a picture of a butterfly that I noted was "the symbol of my hoped-for freedom." I cut it out and placed it on my wall.

After rollerblading with Tynnker, I went out with Stella to several bars and after-hours clubs and didn't return to my apartment until noon the next day. Stella was with me and we decided to take a nap together. Our rest was disturbed when Tynnker pounded on the door to usher me out to go rollerblading. I introduced her to Stella whom she both liked and was immediately jealous of. The three of us spent the next two afternoons and that evening together. Stella refused to buy rollerblades, and Tynnker complained that we weren't using ours, leaving me feeling compromised, wanting to abandon both of them, and hide in my room. The night after my night out with Stella ended with Tynnker sleeping on my extra cot. She told me her wish would have been to seduce Stella, who was straight. Senorita Belinda found out that Tiynnker had spent the night. She later angrily demanded that I pay rent for an additional person in my room, which "made me feel I had broken the law." Tynnker's boyfriend had also called her apartment early that morning and left a message condemning her for spending the night with a model boy. Though "neither of us even nearly exposed ourselves," I later wrote, we were both shamed enough that our friendship immediately cooled and shortly thereafter deteriorated. Within a week of declaring my freedom as a bisexual, I again clung to my religion with the excuse that the partying brought out my homosexuality, and I was rightfully afraid to lose control. My bisexuality was just the latest phase, I concluded yet again.

I'mGrowingLikeA 16
TyrannosaurusRex

During my period of flourishing revelation and celebration about my bisexuality with Tynnker, I was finishing the book *Candide, Or Optimism*. Just after Tynnker and I abandoned one another out of shame, I began *Les Miserables*—the wretched poor. As my time in Spain progressed, I became more famous than I ever would elsewhere for the entirety of my modeling career, while the conflicts I experienced with money, alcoholism, and denial continued. On some level, I must have known that I was on the edge of a precipice in the self-discovery that I fought for. I wrote in my journal that I was "growing like a Tyrannosaurus Rex." Two weeks after declaring my bisexuality and one week after denying it, I increased my gay quotient with a complex formula of 40/40/20—40% gay, 40% bisexual, and 20% pushing me to that Miss Right, "the girl I would marry some day, have kids with, and please my family."

Continually poor—at one point down to a quarter—I maintained my refusal to use the last credit left to borrow on my credit card so that I at least had a few hundred dollars in case I needed a one-way ticket back to Detroit. My mother and grandmother were becoming more vociferous about my returning, if not for good, at least for Easter and Mom's birthday in mid-April (mom also maintained an 800 number in case I didn't have enough money to call and needed a one-way ticket home). In an effort to pull myself out of my financial rut, I called Beatrice in Milan and demanded the money they still owed me for the big Coveri and Stephanel jobs I had done the previous November—four months before. The booker I spoke with put Beatrice, the Diva namesake herself, on the phone, who accused me of "questioning their honor in paying models." She told me that I should get other agencies to find me work. I replied I did. She said the money would come the next day—it didn't. What followed was a kindly worded fax from me requesting only the money I asked for and not the rest of my nearly million lira in unpaid money be sent, as I distrusted the entire money wiring system between agencies. Eventually some of the money came.

I went to my Spanish agency, which I had come to realize was struggling as well, ate three oranges and drank coffee for a meal, and asked for help. I was given some money, which I was told would continue to be parceled out (in smaller sums) about once per week. After this, I went to the bathroom, looked at myself in the mirror and said, "Fuck it, I'm going to do it; I'm going to seriously give it my all; I'm going to go for the gold medal—only I can hold myself back and I won't." I told my bookers that I liked Spain and really wanted to stay, which livened everybody up. This surprised them, since they had thought that I was "pooh-poohing Spain"—and they were right until that point. Immediately they rewarded me with a job.

The job was for Nenuco, a baby products company. I spent three hours in a darkened studio with three babies (and their mothers) who were the lucky co-models. The room was chilly, and I was wearing nothing but a towel to show off my torso and appear as if I had come out of a shower. A small heater barely did enough to keep me warm. One by one, a mother would hand me her baby whom I held in my arms and cradled. The babies, initially incredibly easy to work with, eventually started to fidget in my cold hands. When one cried, another baby replaced the first in a continuous rotation. I was luckily in terrific shape from working out in the park, which made continually holding babies for three hours less difficult. The client enjoyed working with me and kindly gave me copies of the Polaroids.

After this, I agreed to have one drink with Stella. It turned into an all-night binge I once again could not comprehend. Using the approach of Easter, and the resultant acne breakout as additional motivators, I promised myself to hunker down even harder. I abstained, exercised, slept and ate well for one week. Left without a support network to ease me through my withdrawal, my emotional response to my abstinence was bewilderment, depression, and confusion. While thousands of miles away from my California home, I felt for a moment that I suddenly woke up and "wondered what the fuck I was doing on a bus going to a casting somewhere." Sitting alone in my room playing solitaire just as I had in my cubicle at HP, I quickly became bored, frustrated that there was "no justice or fairness in the world," and angry at myself for being a "fuck up." But as I had done so many times before, and would do so many times again in my fight against my excruciating alcoholism, I told myself "I am really just addicted to *using* some form of mind altering substance, not *abusing* it," which cleared the way for me to party again until five the next morning.

The jobs continued, however, and I soon had one with El Corte Ingles, the largest and most distinguished department store in the country. I felt badgered at the shoot, resulting in awakened fears that the photographer, make-up artists, and assistants, who I considered to have "major attitudes," were judging me as being gay. Within days of this, however, my editorial spread from my first week in Madrid, came out in the magazine insert of *El Pais* newspaper to its six million readers. I was concurrently in the March edition of the American version of *GQ* (I had also been in February's). I performed in my first television commercial—for Iberia Airlines. Acknowledging that I was ready for larger markets where I could perhaps earn more of a living, I submitted the tear sheets from the *El Pais* job to my London and Paris Agencies. London thanked me, and Elite replied to my submission and request for return with the following fax:

DEAR ROBERT,

HOW ARE YOU??? THANK'S VERY MUCH FOR SENDING US YOUR NEW T-SHEETS. IT'S VERY GOOD FOR YOUR BOOK, YOU KNOW THAT IT'S MUCH MORE EASY TO WORK WITH T-SHEETS.

FOR THE MOMENT, PARIS MARKET IS SLOW: MARCH WAS
TERRIBLE !!!!!!!!
ANYWAY, WE KEEP IN TOUCH FOR THE FUTURE, IF IN
MADRID YOU CAN STAY AND MAKE SOME MONEY OVER
THERE, YOU SHOULD STAY FOR A MOMENT.
ANYWAY LET ME KNOW WHAT YOU DECIDE TO DO.

HAVE A GREAT TIME
BIG KISS FROM EVE AND VALERIE
ALL MY BEST J-DAVID

Trapped, I turned to nature, which evoked a sublime spirituality
for me. That day, I walked by the Ritz Carlton Hotel on what I described
as "the freshly budded, leafy green path of Paseo de Recotetos." Just
as I was passing "a most beautiful part" of the trail, I "smelled flowers
from the curbside flower vendor and got a hard-on because it was so
beautiful. Hard-ons are caused by other things," I concluded. I then
worked out, went back to my residence and masturbated to something
called "the Fall Attraction." This wasn't all that rewarding, so after
showering, I decided to masturbate again. This time I apparently "got
off to thoughts I once had of Petey and I living and loving together."
Once again disturbed and confused, I smoked two joints and wrote
down the questions: "Where do these twisted thought come from?
Love?…Why do I feel so attached to Petey then so angry with him
especially in sobriety?…So what the fuck do I really feel?" That weekend
was Easter, the holiday I loved the most, the celebration that embraced
new beginnings. I sought a spiritual answer by leaving town.

On Good Friday, I took a train to the ancient, spiritual city of
Toledo. Toledo was not only a cultural Mecca in its day, but also a place
where, during an extensive period known as La Convivencia—the co-
existence—Jews, Christians, and Muslims lived together in harmony.
On the train, I met a lovely Norwegian girl and her mother. She was
23 or 24 and a year or two older than Stella and Tynnker. The girl's

father was a minister, and the girl would keep in touch with me by writing letters and sending pictures for some time to come. Together we visited a synagogue and then attended mass at the main cathedral. After drinking sangria, we watched the Passion Festival, which was composed of a procession of men clad in white robes who looked like the Ku Klux Clan. They carried a platform with a horrific statue of a crucified Jesus Christ on it. I felt aghast.

The next day back in Madrid, despite receiving a cute "miss you" stickie note from Stella, I told her to "piss off" since I had determined she, Tynnker, and a male friend of hers were all "part of a sexually-frustrating, co-dependent, alcoholic love triangle that I wanted no part of." Instead of partying with any of them, I accepted an invitation from my new friend and her mother and walked to the Botanical Café to meet them. There the mother bought me a martini. We then walked to what we convivially called our Easter dinner, a fabulous paella with sangria, and an after-dinner aperitif.

It was there that the mother, who called herself a therapist, told me that what men did to women sexually was "a violent thing that had to do with aggressive, animalistic tendencies." Perhaps, I thought, that was why I felt inhibited to do this violent act on my female friends, and therefore focused more on "the narcissistic part of me" in wanting to do it to men. She continued by telling me that at first she thought I should be a comedian, but had changed her mind, and more recently thought that I should be a minister. Having forgotten that I already shared this with the Arab salesman at the flea market, I later wrote that she was the first person (besides God) that I shared this with. After dinner, we all went to a stimulating live performance of the incredibly athletic, male Russian dancers at the Theatro de Madrid. I shouted and felt "the euphoria of the machismo of the Russian dancers" and good about "the freedom and respect" the two women gave me "to make decisions right or wrong." That night, my subconscious ruined my hetero-acting day as I dreamt that I masturbated on the floor of my teenaged bedroom while thinking of the boy who I had modeled with for the *El Pais* job.

I rollerbladed to the park to exercise alone on Easter Sunday. There I saw a group of men (I noted as "a semi-pro Argentinean, a Nigerian, four Peruvians, and a Columbian") playing soccer. The men invited me to join them, and I agreed. The result was what I considered the best Easter of my life—I won 200 pesetas. The feeling I described was "victory in every pulse of my body, my brain core, its edges, my scalp and down my back through my legs, (where I had had all those pains as a child) to my feet and down my arms, to bring warm blood to my cold hands. My shoulders, which had drawn in pull(ed) back." Apparently feeling "cocky about my skills," I then switched to the losing team to help them out and lost 100 of my pesetas. I played for four or five hours until I was too hungry to play any longer. "Encouraged, respected, and invited back," I later wrote "I am man, capable responsible for making decisions and worthy of being a member of the team of men in the world."

That week, I took my pittance of an advance and faxed Elite, again telling them that I loved Spain, but still wanted a recommendation of where to go to make money. I bought *Death in the Afternoon* and *The Odyssey;* worked out in the park; and went to the Prado museum, where I prayed to a painting of Jesus to guide me as to where to go next, and apologized for not being a better Christian. I then forgave myself for "all the decisions I had ever made in my life" because "I made them with the best information I could possibly have had and for the right reasons given my feelings at the time."

That night I dreamt that I was in a game show. I received a card that said "Love" on it. A girl who looked like Cosette from *Les Miserable* had one that said "Money" on it, which she offered in exchange for mine. Feeling as if I had all the love I needed from my mother and grandmother, but not enough money, I determined that I could give away my Love for the Money. The audience was shocked, which made me rethink what I was doing. The next morning I received my second response from Elite:

179

DATE 08/04/94

DEAR ROBERT,

THANKS VERY MUCH FOR YOUR FAX. JUST TO LET YOU
KNOW THAT A LOT OF MARKETS ARE SLOW AT THE
MOMENT. IN PARIS IT'S TERRIBLE !!!! IN LONDON A MODEL
TOLD US 2 DAYS AGO THAT HE HAD 1 CASTING FOR THE
WEEK.
WE SUGGEST YOU TO KEEP GOING ON THE SPANISH
MARKET; YOU SHOULD GO IN BARCELONA TO MEET A
COUPLE OF AGENCIES, I'M SURE YOU WILL HAVE SOME
GOOD RESPONSE.

WE KEEP IN TOUCH
ALL MY BEST
J-DAVID

Upset and stuck, once again I took a train to another ancient,
historic city—Segovia. There amidst the Roman ruins, Gothic
cathedrals, a temple founded by the Knights Templar, and the famous
Alcazar, the castle-palace of the kings, I prayed for "the Spanish
people, humility, and success." Once again, in a better disposition,
after finishing reading *Les Miserables*, I concluded that all was right
with the world—my meals of canned tuna, I decided, made me happy.
Why, however, was I seemingly always predestined to fail? Obviously,
because "I lacked the will to succeed," I realized, and then came to the
profound conclusion that "my fear is not of failure, but of success."

I dreamt that night of a monster attacking, marring, and
silently killing two boys in the woods. Unfortunately feeling that if
I had success I might misuse it ("like a tyrant") I acted on another
conjecture: that my modeling worries were also really performance

180

issues—"performance with women sexually and with men over sports and career." That Sunday, a week after my Easter Sunday glory, I decided to go back to the soccer field and play another game of football, with detrimental effects. I did not play with my acquaintances of the prior week, but played instead with a group of Peruvians. We all drank while we played and more heavily afterwards. Having not practiced, or ever played other than one time in my life the past week, I wasn't in the best of form. At one point, I embarrassed myself by kicking the ball to a team member from the opposing side.

Despite the humiliation, I apparently won another 100 pesetas. One of the guys mocked me when I played up my impoverishment. This was the same reaction from the other team, when a teammate made fun of my joking about how few pesetas I had. This time I took it as laughing behind my back. I ventured away to drink at a bar. A man I described as "a little self conscious, maybe also homosexual, short, fat boy" befriended me and paid for more beers. His friends joined in, buying me even more. We all left together. I put on my rollerblades, wished everyone *adieu* and immediately fell onto the pavement to everyone's uproarious laughter. I brushed myself off and tried again, but I was so drunk I couldn't balance or maneuver. Nonetheless, I managed to rollerblade home dangerously through the potholed and hilly, busy streets of the capital. I later wondered how I—"the STAR," who was "tall, handsome, athletic, fit and cool"—could befriend such "a little loser" and become a "lost, drunk, stumbling fool, with a skinned knee gotten dishonorably feeling empty and full of self hatred and hatred for God in a way and so many other(s) around me." "The weird, discriminating, negative looks I get from society only makes me feel more associated with the little loser, and more like a rebel," I concluded. Between writing these comments and others in my journal and lying on my bed, I once again wrote and experienced the torturous, empty feelings in my gut that I had shortly before first joining Alcoholics Anonymous two years before.

Once again, I had reached the level of personal misery that had driven me to surrender and seek help in San Diego. This time, however, there was no friendly employer to finance my recovery. Within two days of my emotional anguish, I got three very selective jobs, which indicated that my new modeling career was an incredible success. One was to model for an editorial section of a very high fashion, sexually charged men's magazine, *Moda 16*. Another was to shoot a catalog, once again for El Corte Ingles, and with the outstanding photographer who produced the editorial story that originally launched me into the amazing commercial and pictorial success I received in Spain. The third was for another respected photographer. The agency had to turn down this third shoot because it was to shoot the same day as the El Corte Ingles catalog—so popular was I that jobs were actually turned down.

The spread in *Moda 16*, entitled "Our Neighbor's Fashion," exhibited the designs of Portugal. I worked with two "boys," one of whom I became obsessed with because I could tell he was gay and he turned me on. I did nothing about it except excitedly hold onto his shoulder for too long after a shoot was finished. I felt shamed afterward. At the end of that day, I rollerbladed to one of the most beautiful parks in Madrid. There I watched the sunset casting shadows across the manicured hedges. As the temperature cooled, I felt alone and serene, just as I did when I noticed the seasons change back home. I had my camera with me and snapped a picture. In the center of a small plaza stood the same bronze statue of a draped woman holding a mask above her face. But I didn't recognize her, nor did I remember the statement of the clown I had met there when he asked me if I could take my mask off. This time, however, she did not repulse me. Instead, I snapped a photo of her, continued in the moment, and went on my way.

The following day, April 13, I worked my first large, thousand-dollar job for the wonderful photographer who had taken my first set of photos for El Corte Ingles. Nothing about it was particularly memorable, but he told me "I did a good job." That day I saw Tynnker again for the last time. She told me all her drama—she was living with both her wealthy boyfriend and model girlfriend and needed to choose between the wealthy boyfriend and becoming a super-model Buddhist, which he disagreed with. In the evening, to end what truly should have been a perfect day for any successful model, I went to the famous bar Pacha where paparazzi apparently snapped my picture as I sat at the VIP table drinking free bottles of *Johnny Walker* and *Tanqueray* with my booker, Falco. Operating in a brown-out—close to a blackout, but not quite there yet—I was fortunate to at least to have recorded the events as they occurred before they were lost to memory.

Journal April 14: *first thing I woke up today, I wanted a joint left over from my day before for two reasons: One because I felt all a fog from so much celebrity yesterday (also learned that the Nirvana lead singer shot himself because he said he didn't want to be famous). I dig it. I enjoy learning how to be a showman, confident in front of people, focused on, filmed, as I'm learning about myself. The second reason was because I was wildly in lust of all night didn't even sleep that well, over that other boy I modeled with yesterday. Masturbated 3 times in the middle of the night and otherwise was really restless. I prayed to God to either let me have him or to make me stop wanting him. So I guess today I wanted to get high to forget about this passion. But if I am to be bi or gay then my level of expectation is super hi. And also I would like to be sober about it, so I know it comes from the inside and not from any bizarre twisted, drunken outer exterior. Also I need to be more comfortable with it and cool with it.*

I was at the apex of my new career though I didn't know it. I had achieved the popularity I had seen with Etienne that first weekend in Paris. I wasn't conscious of it. That day I misinterpreted Kurt Cobain's death. Ironically, I was too fucked up to see that he had died because of a suicide prompted by the same affliction that could also kill me.

ComingToJesusAgain— 17
FloatingSouls&AFallingStar

Eighteen months after my thwarted attempt to come out over my love for Petey, months before this trip, while secretly slipping in and out of sobriety in San Diego, I was guided on a relaxed meditation by my therapist. I was to imagine myself sitting in a room. On either side would be two other rooms, one containing a boy and in another a girl. I was to describe them—the girl was blond and pretty like the cheerleaders I befriended in high school; the boy was athletic, cool, and handsome. She asked me to put all judgment aside and choose between which one of the two I would be intimate with. I thought hard and logically and convinced myself it should be the girl. The session ended with my admitting to being perhaps 10% gay.

In Madrid, shortly after my Easter trip to Toledo, I was still at war with the increased percentage I had admitted to myself and continually haunted by my dreams. Most recently, I dreamt that I was in a room with a boy and a girl on the opposite side of a rock. This time I chose the boy, with whom I had a comeless masturbation session. Afterwards, he rested his head on my belly, where I felt pains of emptiness. Later when I was on the beach with the girl, the boy arrived. The girl left and I stayed with him, which felt OK. I accepted it and was happy to see the boy (even though I thought I should have wanted all three of us to have sex).

That day after a trip to the museum of anthropology, I wrote I felt so "wierded out" by Greek and Roman pottery "with their depictions of homosexuality and war" that "I would choose to follow heterosexuality even if it meant cutting my dick off." Despite my resolve, within days I experienced spiritual, emotional, and physical transformations that set the groundwork for my finally accepting I was gay. Naturally aggrieved by the early stages of another abstinence from pot and alcohol, and worried that the agency was failing and I was going with it, I went to demand some money. Once there, I received a small pittance from their pockets. In the ensuing friendly conversation, one of the bookers suggested that a boy on one of the comp cards was cute and asked me what I thought.

My response was to be offended to the point where "my entire body shook with fear and anxiety that everyone was not only convinced but open to the fact that I was a homosexual." That night I lay awake smoking cigarettes and writing in my journal. I admitted I was willing to run anywhere and in fact had been running from this acknowledgement. This was profound. As unrequited fear continued to rock my foundation, I knew I must come to terms with myself or else all of my fears of failure would come true.

Journal April 20: *God can only love me when I truly love myself, my whole self, and give myself the dignity to do so. I can't hide it. My voice betrays me…So much fear, how can this be pleasant for anyone? I'm afraid people will look up on me and laugh behind my back but they only will if I am deceiving myself because no one else is deceived by me. I must come to terms with this or my failure fears will be realized. It's hard. I'll grant myself that, but I can't shut my butterfly up in the closet.*

Naked, I lay with arms spread open on my bed. I opened my soul to Jesus, but this time to accept all of my pieces for who I was and not to condemn me for having natural feelings that I could not control for other men. "It reminded me of the time I discovered my sexuality," I described. I said; "God, this is yours, my body; thank you for it; do as you please." My sperm, I later wrote, was "white on my hands" and "it seemed alive again." I also wrote "I could not help but feel that through Truth, whatever I am is…good," and "I awoke to see my eyes sparkle with a light that I did not see before." I felt victorious, having acknowledged my true nature to God, and come through a major crisis in my life. "Today I feel complete and free in God," I concluded.

Unfortunately my usual doubt set in—my acceptance, I noted,

must have "made me start to notice girls more." My neighbor, Hernan, and I would talk about girls and how much we missed having a girlfriend Hernan was a native Madridian and what I considered a normal guy who was studying for a qualifying exam and lived next door. "If all was right in the world, why did I chain-smoke so many cigarettes," I questioned in my journal. "Why did I feel such compulsive NEED? For What?" And "why did I still not have enough pesetas?" I yearned for answers.

Having no one to help me understand what it meant to be a gay or even a bisexual man, and having only imagined bad stereotypes to rely on, I searched for solace and meaning wherever I could. One afternoon while sitting and reading on "a green field during a purple sunset," I imagined the figure of my father sitting calmly behind me, smoking a cigarette as if he were observing and protecting me. While waiting outside for a casting, I saw a shooting star, which I interpreted to mean that quick movements or false starts would be bad for me. There would always be problems, I concluded, as day ended. Where I went or what I did was "up to God."

One night, after the Senorita went to bed, a guy apparently switched the TV to a channel showing three men and one woman fucking. While I was somewhat erotically stimulated, it disturbed me. Homosexuality was obviously "as normal as a hangover" in Spain. That night, I dreamt that a black wolf was chasing me, causing me to hide behind the jeweled cloak of a woman during the attack. As a child, I had also dreamt of a black wolf that chased me through a department store. When I tried to get away the stairwell suddenly twisted upside down, preventing me going further, and leaving me in harm's way. My grandmother, as if in heaven, reached out her arm to help me up.

In Madrid, my straight friend Hernan had recently made a quip about a girl who accidentally rubbed her boob across his arm. "Watch out, I'm dangerous," he had said to her. Perhaps, I reasoned, from this and my dream, the Wolf was me—"I was running away from the aggressor in me." Perhaps I was the victim in all of my homosexual experiences. After all, wasn't homosexual sex an aggressive act by one aggressor and one "conquered"? To be the aggressor, as I longed to be, would be "corrupt," I once again decided in great confusion. Only with a woman could it mean "enduring love." Nonetheless, the seed had been planted for further understanding.

It was nearly six months after my thirtieth birthday, 330 days in Europe, and one month short of the year goal I had set for myself. I knew from experience that the modeling season would soon die during the upcoming summer, and that my very survival continually was in question. I called both my mother and the Homeowners Association president (who had the task of dispersing the remainder of my abandoned belongings). My lack of money, pressure from my family to return, and need to clean up the mess I had left, was weighing on me. But Spain was holding me for a reason, I thought—"God, or the invisible hand that moves me won't until I'm strong enough to go." I had learned a lot and had much more to learn. I believed in myself and in what I was doing. I knew I had the power to control my own life and make it a happy one. I wrote, "Fuck the furniture, fuck the left over CD's, fuck the debt, and fuck the statement from my 87 year old grandmother who told me that she didn't believe in me or what I was doing." I would stick it out.

The next two days I ended up working two of the most amazing and high-paying jobs of my career—a commercial for Gallerias, the second (behind El Corte Ingles) of the two great department store chains of Spain. In addition to being joyful and eccentric, the job seemingly poked fun at the conservative businessman that I was so desperately seeking a respite from. The first day I gleefully danced for three hours in a suit and tie, which was fun, but the next day was extraordinary. It was shot on the cordoned-off blocks directly outside the Atocha Train Station, which was the largest station in the country where thousands were transported every day. Cameras, booms, lighting, and a large crew stood readied as passersby watched. Wearing nothing but a swimsuit over my well-defined body and a watch, while carrying a briefcase, I pretended to be walking and then hopped onto a trampoline as I briefly looked at my watch. In a second scene, wearing only another tight-fitting bathing suit, a watch, goggles, and a swim cap, I walked in the opposite direction to 50 extras dressed in formal business suits and ties.

In the days that followed, I noticed people seemed to stare at me in the streets. "Girls fell into major giggles" when I smiled at them. My job was moving at the right speed, I was convinced, but I was still lonely. The day after my big job, I called Petey collect, but don't know if I ever talked to him. I then sat alone in my room on "a bright, sunny, hot day, drinking wine and thinking how grateful I was." I looked outside the lacey, white curtains, and through the old, white painted French doors, beyond the gardenia plants hanging on the Spanish wrought iron fence, and noted "the white seeds of spring are floating down in such abundance as to appear as snow falling." I sketched a picture of the scene. I later wrote "I am teary eyed, I have drank wine and eaten bread alone today in my room in memory of my Lord"—I further "proclaimed my weariness and desire to forfeit all life for that which is, and is to come, in Jesus Christ and in His father, God, my God." I then wondered "if the fluffy white flowing seeds are souls taking a trip in the wind."

The eventual decline of my career started soon after this. I woke up and went to work out in the park where the smell of the morning flowers made me nostalgic for summer and home. I heard a military band play in the distance. That afternoon, after finishing Hemingway's *Death in the Afternoon,* I went to a casting for the famous photographer, Michael Wray, who I discovered felt challenged to photograph me as well as Louis del Amo (my original *Sin Barriers* photographer) had done. He awarded me the job to start the next day. After the casting, I took a melancholic walk in a beautiful nearby park. In the midst of a shallow pool stood an ancient Egyptian temple called the Temple of Debod. It was originally built to honor Isis, the Goddess of Magic and Giver of Life, and Amon, who at one time was one of the most important deities in ancient Egypt but then faded into obscurity—the temple had been gifted to Spain. Overcome with the magnificence of the structure, I prayed to Jesus, imagining that I was splashing my face in the water and being cleansed. Feeling much as I had after taking communion, and knowing my propensity to fuck myself up afterwards, I gave the intent "if the military band I had heard earlier were to march by and shoot me, it would be okay." But a convenient death could not save me from my experiences or lessons to come.

The job the following day was the worst of my entire modeling experience, would be my last job in Spain, and would signify the slow and fitful demise of my modeling career—the falling star was indeed symbolic of more than I had thought it to be. Nervous from excessive binging and recoveries, I worked for nine grueling hours during which I felt "taunted, harassed, challenged, and intimidated" to perform for a photographer who could not be pleased. Instead of the luxurious designer clothes I had worn on my first shoot, the clothes I wore reminded me of something I was forced to wear as a Hewlett-Packard employee. Instead of feeling sophisticated, I felt dowdy. The more the photographer ignored any sense of humanity in his interaction with me, the more I recoiled in self-loathing. Yet he continued to bark disapprovingly to show him all I had, while his demoralizing tone that day made me feel "ugly, ashamed, and frighteningly confused." Instead of positive, confident thoughts, fears arose every time I heard the shutter click. I wondered what was to become of my lost possessions, as the camera flashed. What would happen to all my straight friends if I were to come out as gay? I became horrified. What would my mom think if I told her I didn't think it was possible to produce grandchildren? How would I be treated by society when everyone knew I was a hated fag I questioned. I left the job walking aimlessly into the fading light that, although it cast long shadows, reminded me of the hot brightness of the Tokyo sun the day I drank too much absinthe. Everything was too cruelly clear. Every rock, pebble, and hole in the pavement seemed to berate me as I stared down, too frightened to make eye contact with any passerby.

That night I dreamt that I was hanging out with both my father and his father—both of whom died very early—and how wonderful it was for us, three generations of Reinckes together. The following evening, sitting alone in a bar drinking what I counted as six beers, I judged the barman. I criticized him for being transformed by his own drinking and thereby having "given up his hope." Feeling guilty for my inability to help him, I oddly responded by not tipping him. As days progressed, I observed correctly that I felt disassociated. I exercised fervently, and craved hash, but did not smoke it. Overwhelmed by fear, my voice quivered with nervous anxiety. I was too paralyzed even to look at my photos from the Fendi and Fusco shows that had recently come out in the *Uomo* collections. Desperate, I again wrote that I was destined to fail unless I could control this overwhelming fear.

By Tuesday May 10, the day that apparently "sprang from Hell," I walked to the agency to get more money. The accountant was there and we argued. I had worked out my earnings and showed him that even after agency fees, advances, rent and flight were deducted, the agency owed me more money. Despite this, he only paid me less than I had received when the bookers had given me cash from their own pockets (1,000 Pasetas). Later, drunk and enraged, I no longer cared if I got work or not. I purposefully flubbed a casting, smoked cigarettes "suicidally," suddenly disliked my friend next door, who was "sacrificing his life to study for an exam he didn't know he'd pass," and even the girl on the other side of me, who I described as "a Yugoslavian too fat to work in Madrid."

I worked out in my journal that the only reason I had fear was "BECAUSE I AM IN CHARGE." The next day I told the agency I was leaving, to buy me an airplane ticket and to give me the remainder of my money (they bought me the ticket and gave me half). I called Elite and told them that I was coming back to Paris and to give me the best date (we set it for two-weeks). I further told Elite to find me a place to live, which they did. I called the homeowners association woman in San Diego and told her to sell every stick of my furniture NOW. She had already given away most everything I owned—couches, chairs, my waterbed, dishes, microwave, books, stereo system—and had sold only a few items for which she received very little money.

Afterwards I got drunk and spent the money that the agency had given me the prior day on a rock of hash. It turned out that the hash in a bag really was a rock. It was stupid, and I should have looked at it first, and I decided that God did not let me buy it. I comforted myself back at the hostel by watching the solar eclipse with my neighbor Hernan and finishing the second volume of *Les Miserables*. My brain was a scrambled, confused mess, and all I had was faith, I noted in my journal that day, and sketched another picture of a cross. The next day I started reading my new book, Machiavelli's *The Prince,* and walked to a church where I "prayed, kissed my hands, and touched them to the foot of a statue of a crucified Jesus in symbolic ritual of my thankfulness for his blessings." Influenced by my readings and an overwhelming sense of hopelessness, I hit another emotional bottom.

Just when I thought I was emotionally and financially dead, a letter arrived from my mother. Hewlett-Packard owed me $7,000, which represented the cash-out of my pension that I had requested, and it was on its way. I thanked Jesus and started working on my tax return to see if I couldn't get more. Despite what I had come to know as true about myself, body and soul, I convinced myself that I was successful at one thing: having moved away from my homosexual desires, tendencies, and fear. Drugs were responsible for bringing them out in the first place; gays ran the business, but I was already in the club; I would not suck anyone's dick to be famous; and, finally, I was to watch out for people who assumed that I was gay.

A week before my return to Paris, the countdown was on. Much reminiscent of Tokyo, I took myself out, smoked pot publicly, drank everywhere and everything from martinis to Jack Daniels neat, and spent my last days with random fashion industry strangers who had little bearing on my world. Six days before Paris I went out on the town

191

to a huge party at Pacha, Madrid's most famous club, getting stoned with other models in the club and drinking champagne. I made out with a girl named Theona (or Pheona) on the dance floor, who supposedly, "like all the boys and girls," was "willing or wanting some sort of sexual thing." At some point, a rich man passing through to Uruguay from the Gran Prix in Monte Carlo kissed me and someone else on the hand and then went off singing "Singing in the Rain." Another girl blew me kisses and told me to call her and we'd do something fun. I unsuccessfully called her once, and instead, relentlessly obsessed about a hot model named Ben who seemed too much "the man" to be gay. Two days later, as I awoke at 5:30 p.m., the club promoter stopped by my hostel and personally handed me an invitation to "an amazing reggae party." I listed the pros and cons to going out again, which included my reputation with the agency, the hostel, and, in fact, the whole city would change and I would not be able to "deny it" to self or friends—"but why deny what?" I had written in the margin. Fearfully, I managed to stay in that night only. I went out a couple days later to a dinner party that was held in my honor by Pacha, with super-hot Ben and twelve crazy models, whose phantom names and descriptions are jotted down in my notes but who I don't have the slightest recollection of. Apparently, the partying included flaming shots and dancing at another club until 7:30 the following morning. I left for Paris three months after I arrived in Spain, many weeks longer than the two weeks I expected, with definitive internal growth despite my self-sabotage. Growth that could only conclude where my trip began—in Paris.

ILoveCock 18

I arrived in Paris late Tuesday afternoon, an early spring day of May 24, almost exactly one year after I first arrived. I took a taxi from the Charles de Gaulle airport directly to the Rue St. Claude and the apartment that Elite had assigned me. There I was to meet my new roommate, a non-model girl, and get established.

I left the cab directly in front of a five-story building, most likely built in the early twentieth century but evocative of the late Empire period complete with the facade of wooden shutters on each of the French windows. The area was considered one of the best places to live in Paris and contained a host of small, wonderful cafés, boulangeries, wine shops (which I luckily couldn't afford), small food markets of every category and the nearby, Sunday Bastille farmers' market. Sitting squarely in the Third Arrondissement, my building also was near the famed Picasso Museum, walking distance to the Louvre, and bounded by the Pompidou Center on one side, and the Place de la Republic (where the new Opera was housed) on the other. Most significant of all, the apartment was located in the ancient Marais District, which was the center of the Paris gay community.

Anxious to approach this newest Parisian episode with the Machiavellian concept that life was "war with courtesy" (and to make a good impression on my new roommate) I took a moment to pause at the first-floor café located directly below my new apartment building in order to strategize. I bought myself a civilized cup of espresso and a pack of cigarettes and pulled out my journal to make some notes of how I was to behave, remembering that I was now entering a new surf break and would have to stay on the outside—beyond the prime breaking point where the locals were—until I understood it better. "Gaining enlightenment from cathedrals" while there, I was also to be "cautious of homosexuals."

Completing my journal, I walked around the side of the building, located the buzzer, buzzed Madeleina-Karoline—MK—and walked my way up the five flights of winding stairs (the building like many in France had no elevator to the top and fifth floor). The door was open and I stepped into a miniscule foyer, where my new roommate greeted me. Wearing her customary penny loafers, oxford shirt, and khaki pants, she made an effort to smile and greeted me with a chuckle of sorts and a handshake.

I laid my things down and began the tour. The first room on the right was the kitchen. Clean and recently upgraded with new tile and a tiny cabinet over the oven, it was relatively large compared to Eve's kitchen corner, well stocked, obviously used and had a small oven/range and sink that was set as low as the one in Tokyo. While standing in the kitchen, MK—who was an administrator for a small office of the Assembly Nationale—manipulated the conversation to turn to sex. She made a clear and succinct point in her excellent but highly accented English to tell me that she was a bisexual—a "bee-sex-youuu-el." Without hesitation, I responded that I was one too. I felt absolutely no hypocrisy from the list of rules I had just made in the café downstairs, nor in my comfort in knowing my new roommate was bisexual. She seemed obviously relieved that that was said. Later she confided in me that she liked to rent her room out to Elite male models in the hopes of finding a boyfriend. This seemed odd coming from her, as she seemed so casually masculine.

The tour moved into her bedroom, which contained her unmade bed composed of two thin mattresses placed directly on the floor. The bed and the sparseness of her room were in direct contrast to the otherwise picture-perfect, French quaintness of the rest of the apartment. Also in her room was the only shower, which was a traditional large bathtub with a plastic curtain surrounding it, with a moveable showerhead. The sink stood next to that, and I have no memory if the toilet was also there or elsewhere.

We finally made it into my room, which was as ideal as I could have possibly hoped for. On one wall was a little fireplace, unusable, but it had a wonderful, decorative, and white painted mantle complete with candles and incense sticks. A cream-colored sofa, a chair, and a small table stood against the opposite wall. A tall window opened to a great view of the avenues and tiny streets below, and directly onto the neo-Baroque church next door (with cross on its steeple that I could see from my room). It had a small balcony as well, where I could sneak cigarettes, although MK despised them. My bed, which was a twin, was nicely made up with fresh sheets and also served as a seating area.

A console table in the hallway folded out to a dining room table, which could be moved to my room, where MK and I would host some of our dinner parties. Together we would make fabulous dinners of a meat dish, cheeses, fresh fruit, coffees, and a precursory salad. Our first night together was celebrated with a simple rendition of this. MK had a great stereo, and that night I contributed the modeling-evocative music of the Stereo MCs as we ate and talked.

The following day was equally welcoming. Girls on the subway took a photo of me, which gave me confidence I was still gorgeous. An old woman gave me 10 Francs for a candle at a church, which bode well for the spiritual, giving nature of the French. The sun cooperated too, and I found that I could sit in my room by my open window and sun myself through the French doors. Later that evening I met Eve at the Frog & Rosbif, which I had learned to enjoy so much with Celeste, who had taken my photos in February. By the end of that evening, all my initial fears—of my roommate, my agency, and the city—were resolved and I wrote that I was no longer terrorized.

I do not remember if MK was a lawyer or not, but do know that she was quite astute and enjoyed a good debate. Being an intellectual and thinking herself a bisexual at the time, however, meant that she was equally torn between her heart and what she thought was socially appropriate behavior in her head. As an only child like me, MK was constantly challenged to find interesting new ways to entertain herself.

One way she chose to do so was by creating drama and setups for those that came within her circle. I became both a pawn and a consort in her dealings.

Within two days of living in Paris, I ran into beautiful, blond, sexually ambiguous Rusty from my first stay in Milan a year earlier. Rusty became the center of heated conversation about not only his orientation, but how sexy and sensual he was, and what I should do about it. One of MK's favorite words, theories, and concepts was *seduction*—most likely because she was so inept at it. My contribution to our fervent conversation was that, on some level, I realized that I needed to be assertive with a guy and to quit thinking of myself as the victim.

That Saturday, the day after our first dinner party together with all straight friends—including Hugo and his wife—I was invited to dinner with Rusty. I journaled that I accepted, fully intending to let whatever happened, happen. What resulted, I described as "a wild night" and "another breakthrough"—if only in my own mind. Prior to going to Rusty's, I got down on my knees in my room above the church and prayed we would not be led into temptation.

His apartment was near ours—in a superb location and well furnished. Exceedingly large and loft-like for a central Parisian apartment, it was composed of one and a half floors; it was definitely not his. The man who owned it was away, Rusty said. I showed up without wine in order to appear as if our dinner meant little to me. Rusty lit candles and incense and put on some classical music. I smirked to connote my approval of a seduction. My hands sweated profusely. We had a nice dinner and talked about superficialities while I thought of little else other than my desire for him, *please,* to make a move. He didn't. I later walked over to the couch where I perused either a coffee table book or his portfolio.

I later wrote that while I did this, I sat frozen—didn't know what to do. I had prayed for no temptation and there was none—except I did have a hard-on most of the time, which attributed to my paralysis. The night ended like so many prior experiences had when, even though I was relatively conscious, I did not connect my physical reaction or feelings with what was happening or had happened.

Coming home to my room, I looked for my last cigarette—for I was to quit smoking. Even it was missing—"a further symbol of my cleansed life." Both of us must have thought the other gay, I determined ("but he was so deceptive about it, as I am also"). Yet Rusty was "like me, not gay, but sympathetic, and like all of us, with some tendencies or feelings." How ridiculous, I thought, for me to spend so much time worrying about this. And how ridiculous to fall in love with a guy, "to have sex with some dude, and think that would make me happy or in the least bit fulfilling."

For weeks thereafter, Rusty would lose his identity as a human being and become nothing more than a pretty conversation piece between MK and I to consider if he were gay and how I could seduce him. On one other occasion, in which we hosted a dinner party for only him in the hope that I could seduce him, he invited a friend also named Robert who completely fouled our attempt—perhaps as a "fuck you." The final photo I have of him has just such a gesture.

The following morning, Sunday, I went off to church and communion at the American Cathedral of Paris. There I apparently met a girl named Debbie of whom I haven't the slightest recollection. After having lunch with her and drinking Russian vodka, we apparently, according to my journal and Franklin, had sex. She wanted me to spend the night but I told her I was tired and could not. "A cat was going crazy in the hallway" and "I was going crazy in my head." Debbie was the tenth woman I had some form of sex with, which I added to four men on my tally sheet. Why did I do this, I asked. I must have been trying to prove my manhood to everyone and me, and to discipline myself more, I reasoned.

I then had another nightmare. It was nighttime, and I was in the playroom I had as a boy and suddenly felt spooked. I knew I would be killed, so I ran. I tried to make it to the neighbor girl's house two houses down, but only made it to the next-door girl whom I had kissed as an early teen out of peer pressure and presumed duty. I rang the bell but no one answered. The monster—a huge, scary, and mean man—came around the other side by the front and grabbed me. I pretended all was cool and said, "Oh let me kiss you," and then I kissed him on the lips. "Big, powerful, and oppressive," he dragged me by the collar. I didn't know if he was going to torture me or eat me alive. "I pretend I wanted him sexually." I told him, "Let me kiss you," again while feeling appalled and not wanting to. And then I woke up.

My casting that morning was for a marriage magazine. The next day, I went out with Eve to the movies and dinner. I disclosed to her, possibly in an attempt to defend not wanting to have sex, all about both my gay and straight experiences. It didn't work. I later wrote: **Journal June 3:** *Writing by the light of a left candle on the fireplace mantel of my Paris apartment. Rose incense burns besides it. A warm rain from the heavens sooths the night. Sunday and Tuesday I celebrated life. I shared my experiences with women, Gods beautiful, gracious gift to the universe. After telling Eve of my homo and other heterosexual experiences she has unprotected sex with me. Tonight, I masturbated on the terrace in the rain. I am free…I constantly all day long think about sex. I am a sexual being. I feel happy. Free here to speak openly of my past, of my bisexual nature and still getting more and more. Because I'm honest, because I'm real. Because I'm free. Now I must focus on getting and wanting work.*

The initial withdrawal from partying in Madrid had worn off, with the customary feelings of being lost and confused followed by growing unmitigated clarity. MK told me I owed rent. The agency was neither paying for it, nor fronting it. They simply didn't do this, they told me, except for very high-paying female models, but never for men. To make matters more difficult, they took 64% of all job income— but they did pay their models promptly, unlike everywhere else. One solution was to file the taxes I had begun in Madrid so that I could get a refund. I started in on it again. I then journaled that my goal was three jobs a week, as if some force would note this and magically make jobs available.

Before I knew it, it was Friday again and I found myself going out with MK to her favorite, and the best, lesbian bar in the city—Le Privilege. Drinks were relatively costly and certainly not free to a male model, so I drank sparingly. MK also influenced me by her relatively small amount of drinking—though she occasionally enjoyed a toke or two from the pot I bought. This, along with the high cost of wine, gave me a relatively long spell of clear thinking. The rainy weekend that followed also contributed by giving me some quiet, peaceful days at home eating good meals and living a decent and moderate life. By mid-week, however, my clearing mind caused me more trouble.

I had another dream; this time of an "invasion of body snatchers." While I stood in a building, a bunch of zombie-like people came after me and the other "normal ones." I determined that I would stand my ground. Two zombie men approached me and wanted to kiss me. I ran away down some stairs and out the guarded open door into the sunlight between the building and a McDonald's restaurant. I felt I needed to stay out in the light but did not want to separate from the masses of normal people for fear of attack. I awoke traumatized.

Coincidentally, that evening, MK had another of her dinner parties, which reminded me of the dream. This time one of her best friends, who looked like Beethoven, complete with full, bushy hair and squat stature, attended. He had a girlfriend, but claimed—perhaps just for MK and I—to be a bisexual. Another man came as well, who I mistakenly wrote in my journal was the same name, Michael Wray, as the last photographer who shot and traumatized me in Madrid. He, too, was gay or bisexual and as unappealing to me as the other.

At one point during dinner, one of the two unpleasant guests shouted at me that he wanted more scotch. I immediately popped up to get him some. I later wrote that I wondered how this bisexual could be so rude when I knew he was so "wanting, needing, confused, crazy and nice." Did they "hate me because they knew I was bi or gay" and were "jealous of my money, fame and fun?" And "why was I appeasing this crazy man?" Surely, this was "the apex of my codependence—not aware of how I feel but instead with how to appease." Life with a lesbian roommate and all her gay friends in Paris was like *"Invasion of the Body Snatchers,"* I wrote. Yet everything from the collage I had created and placed on my wall "to the way I act, sit, talk, and am, says gay, gay, and gay to everyone that notices. I must be a very selective homosexual and not so selective when it comes to being a heterosexual," I concluded

Still confused, though by lessening degrees, I continued to project my frustration onto my exaggerated drive for a successful, financially lucrative career. Doing what I felt was needed in the grandiose, dramatic manner I was so good at, I went to the agency and told them "I want to be a supermodel...I wasn't there just to survive." The next day they set me up with an agency from Greece—Unique— that I ended up getting (modeling for Unique in Greece would, within a few months, end my European experience). They also pretended with me that a new fresh card would help. The elaborately dressed, perfumed, and bejeweled elderly matron booker, Edith, deigned to help me. While looking at one of my photos, she made the sarcastic comment that I should send it to my grandmother. She then asked me if I liked boys or girls more.

This time, I was undaunted. "Girls," I said, "at the moment." Conveniently, one of the bookers or another model was a palmist and concurred with me that I was a 40/40/20 and a romantic—not a "field player." "Find him a nice girlfriend," the diva proclaimed. Once again having been validated as at least partially straight—this time by the supreme mother—I later that night invited Eve over to dinner and had sex with her—I remember nothing of the event.

The next day, June 14, I was on an airplane to the most lucrative job of my modeling career until that time. It shot in an idyllic resort town in the French Alps, called Annecy where I modeled eight shots per day for a French catalog. The job matched the $1,000 per day of my Spanish job, but shot for two full days. Only my last modeling job shot for *Ski* Magazine 3 ½ years later in Aspen, Colorado, would pay me more.

The wardrobes were brilliant. The town, a perfect French resort, offered amazing backdrops—gorgeous palaces, handsome spanning bridges, long, tree-covered canals, lakes with a backdrop of the Alps. In one very memorable shot I sat in a wooden boat with my arm draped over the edge, wearing fine linen and cotton shirts. In another I walked a stony path in front of a row of outdoor eateries and cafés as the throngs of tourists and locals watched the photo shoot. One afternoon I swam in the lake, and the next we water-skied in it—an activity I was decent at. Our final day there consisted of driving to the outskirts of town amidst the beauty and splendor of fresh, clean air and the most ideally lush green pastures, valleys, and mountain views imaginable.

There in the intimate, beautifully rustic restaurant/home of an elderly couple of men were set up a few, long tables on the inside and a couple more around the porch. The photographer knew the men and we were the only people there. In the middle of the main room was a large stone oven in which bread and pastries were made and food cooked. Everything was provided locally or cooked on site. The dinner served us that evening was one of the best I ever ate. This being France, it consisted of several wonderful courses of cheeses, salad, fresh fruit and pastries, and various wines appropriate to the course served, which I drank cordially like the civilized human being I constantly hoped I was (only later did I get stoned with the stylist, thinking that I was superior to those who didn't). The main dish consisted of a rooster cooked in their outdoor pit for three days so that the meat would be tender and not stringy, which I loved.

I flew back to Paris refreshed, invigorated, and full of hope, to find out the agency was closing its men's division. Elite Hommes, one of the most amazing agencies I would have imagined in the world, was closing. I was not one of the lucky ones whom they took the courtesy of telling in advance, or finding another agency for.

At first I convinced myself that I didn't care, that they didn't push me enough, and that I was going to leave them anyhow. I believed in myself. I was going to go on. "Fuck, fuck, another horrible change," I wrote, after which I got drunk at Le Privilege with MK, Hugo, and his wife.

As days progressed other conflicts emerged as well. My mother and grandmother pleaded with me to return to Michigan, my acquaintance with Rusty was weird and strained, and most troubling of all, MK told me she was attracted to me—a feeling she said she thought she could only have for girls. I told her that "I loved her as a person, a sister, a friend, a fellow intellect, but not as a man and woman sexual couple." Her reactions, I wrote, was to turn into a "moody, cranky, sad bitch."

Realizing I was "not a supermodel, but a hell of a lot more than I was a year ago," I decided it was time to beat the pavement and find a new agency. The problem was, once again and as it had been a year earlier, it was the beginning of the show season and agencies did not want to take me on. The agency Success showed an interest, though offered nothing solid, and MGM was "just blah," as once again I was told I was too short and my book not big or good enough. Making matters worse in my estimation was that my agency wasn't getting all the show castings. Crashing a few, I considered becoming independent and negotiating with clients myself, which was highly improbable since I had no connections.

During the course of one of my castings, I chatted with one of the clients—a man named Fernand, who was a PR man from an agency that supposedly put on five of the big Parisian shows. Fernand seemed to take a genuine interest in me and wanted to help. A couple days after my first meeting with him, he invited me to lunch. The lunch was leisurely and long, taking two or three hours, which told me this man was truly in charge of his own day, and very, very French. At some point, his partner (I wasn't sure if this just meant working partner), who was named Oreo, joined us. By that time, I had already admitted to being a bisexual.

Fernand invited me to a dinner party to be held that evening at Oreo's palatial French apartment. I was told there would be four or five other boys there as well. Though nervous, I thought it would be a good idea. After all, I had continually felt like an outcast to the uper-echelon in the modeling world and this could be my chance to move up. I arrived at the beautifully sized, if not overly elaborate, apartment feeling awkward and strange. I then saw the long table laid out for dinner—for just three. There would be no other guest but me.

Shocked and frightened, I nonetheless stayed and drank three bottles of wine with the twosome. At some point we kissed and then went into the bedroom. I sat on the floor and let Fernand, who I was into, take off my shirt and reach down to my pants. I pushed Oreo aside, finding him not very attractive. We floundered around a bit, but did nothing much. My lack of experience and do-nothingness-while-they-did-it-all didn't seem to be very provocative. I thought perhaps Oreo was jealous of me and not very happy that I pushed him away. The evening ended without much fanfare.

The next day was "hot, hot, hot, and humid." My detoxing exacerbated the effect of the heat. I sweated profusely and felt delirious. After waiting in line an hour and a half for a casting, for which I was told I'd have to take my pants off, and after sitting around in hot room with pretty but horrendously catty male models, I gave up and left. At some point, most likely prior to this, I showed up at Fernand's office or studio, or whatever it was, to pick up the backpack I had brought with me to their apartment at the time, I thought we would have a serious discussion about our dinner party. Fernand asked me how I felt, which I took as being sensitive and a good sign. I asked myself the same question later in my journal. "Crazy" was my honest answer—"it's all very crazy…kind of like another realm."

For the first time since my presumed rejection by the man I loved, which sent me on this journey, I felt excited about having a "boyfriend"—assuming incorrectly that that's what floundering around with Fernand and his "partner" meant. Admittedly, I would have preferred "a more conservative image for a boyfriend," but

Fernand was "okay to me." I had entered what felt like another realm of existence, but I wanted it to be right. I did not want to be looked upon as exploiting Fernand for his contacts. Nor did I want to use him. I didn't know if being public with our affections would benefit or really hurt my career, but in either case, I wished he wasn't even in the industry. I wanted to make it in the industry on my own merit, by my own good looks, and because of my own good representation.

Pleasant days followed, although never again with Fernand. MK and I spent a day in the Marais. In the evening she, her bisexual Beethoven-like friend, his girlfriend, and I had a wonderful dinner, which she called a welcoming of our friendship party, but could have been taken as a coming out dinner party for me. We had our customary cheese plate and then had a ham and potatoes, sesame bread, and a tomato salad. I wrote in my journal that I felt hopeful, optimistic, and happy but did not know why. I felt that time had changed. I was becoming aware of who I was as a human being on this earth and was happy. I was being provided for by God and growing, progressing, and becoming whole and complete again.

Continuing in my feeling of elation, the following day I took my rollerblades and rollerbladed all over the city in the sunlight. I zoomed by the Eiffel Tower and down the Champs Elysees. I journeyed around the "stomach of Paris" (Les Halles), where I had lived with Eve, to the Opera, and then home. That evening, released from and releasing so much pent up angst and fear, I asked in my journal for the next big desire: relief from substance abuse. But this prayer was not answered for another seven years.

Christophe 19

"**F**reaking out" over constantly having to come up with money to pay rent, I walked out of the apartment in order to make some private long distance calls at an outdoor phone booth. I called Beatrice in Milan and Jet Set in Madrid to find out about the money they owed me and perhaps about work. I called airlines, the storage unit in San Diego, and the Visa people—to find out how much money I had left. In the midst of all of this, a sultry, dark-haired, young Parisian boy passed by my bubble of telecommunications.

We made a series of eye contacts. It was quite clear to even me that he wasn't looking for directions or just wanting to make casual conversation—after all, I was behind a glass wall carrying on obviously heated discussions. I remember exiting the phone booth and the conversation being very short, he speaking in broken English. He lived nearby, and, as I understood by his gestures, I was to follow him. I was more silent than was my custom with a stranger, although I'm sure I enlightened him with at least a partial life story, and, at a minimum, that I was a model—as if I had to further sell the inevitable.

His apartment had the feel of a college dorm room and may have been one. I sat on the lower portion of a bunk bed and let him give me a blow and hand job. Although obviously turned on by him and the situation, I have no memory of what he did to himself or if I contributed. I think that whatever happened, it was satisfying for him, because there was a clear conclusion that seemed mutually satisfactory. We walked out without any exchange of phone numbers or follow-up.

That day I had run into Luuk. Luuk had faxed me the day I arrived in Paris—we had been faxing each other since he left Tokyo. We spent some time talking in my apartment, apparently. Unfortunately, I do not recall our conversation, perhaps because I had categorized him firmly as a straight friend. I strongly believed that I couldn't be gay and keep my straight friends, which was an underlying cause of my leaving my home in San Diego. I couldn't come out and be me when I thought that the world and all those who loved me, loved me because I was straight, or would be angry at me or disrespect or judge me for deceiving them. After all, weren't all of these relationships fragile and based upon who they thought me to be? I unfortunately had little room for Luuk.

Coincidentally I also ran into Celeste, the female photographer with whom I had so many intimate conversations at the Frog & Rosbif prior to leaving Paris for Madrid. The following day I also ran into Gregor, my best-friend and former roommate from my post-Tokyo time in Milan, and Luuk walking Gregor's white golden retriever. I knew Gregor lived in Paris and that work was difficult even for him—he had kept in touch, and his wife would continue to do so even after I left Europe—but I was surprised that he too was friends with Luuk, just as I had been surprised about Luuk and Lothar's friendship. I would eventually run into Lothar and Zoë too, although I remember nothing of it.

I, nonetheless, hung out with Gregor that drizzly day and went with him to one of his castings, just as we did in the days after we had lived together. Like the older brother who took care of finding me a new agency in Milan, he put out the same effort in Paris. He introduced me to his agency, Success. My notes later indicate, however, that I thought that Success the agency, like success the concept, would somehow require that I be honest with everybody about my sexuality.

That night Gregor invited me over to his house for dinner and to watch the World Cup soccer championship between his home team, Holland, and Morocco. I unfortunately accepted. The perceived conflict between the random and rewarding jerk-off I had so recently experienced and my daily heterosexual friendships was at an all-time high. Participating in heterosexual camaraderie and brotherly friendship that I thought being openly gay would deny me was not the thing to do. To make matters worse, Gregor as usual produced an excess of hash—even for me—that I smoked liberally, and it resulted in excruciating paranoia.

Also invited was a host of incredibly handsome Dutch male models, who were successful, confident, and comfortable with each other. A beautiful blond boy asked me a question, which triggered, I later wrote, "a passing of pain and discovery of something I would rather not be." After which I "completely lost it." My face became contorted—I could not stop creating an odd smirk—to hide what I felt where the exposed details of every sexual encounter I had had with a man. I blushed with a horrific false sense of shame, and wrongdoing. Gregor seriously questioned my well-being. I excused myself to go to the bathroom where I washed my face with water and continually looked in the mirror, telling myself that I was okay, that it would be okay, that I could go back out there and just, please, act normally.

The game ended, I walked home and opened my journal. I wrote that "The question I have to answer for God, myself and anyone else, is, 'am I gay?'" Trying finally to work out who I was, I, as usual, wrote, "I've explored it and since I ~~like~~ love women I feel right focusing on my heterosexuality." But the hypocrisy had become too much, even for me. Within a couple lines, I asked myself, "what do I fucking feel about being masturbated and sucked by another boy I picked up by the telephones last night?" And my answer was "Relived." But what I wanted (wanted, wanted) was to "fall in love." What I needed most was "passion, compassion, and love."

It was time to make a firm decision to put timidity and naiveté to bed and to grow up. No longer would life consist of me living in a fool's paradise; I would know it as it was—not black and white, but shades of gray. I needed to realize that I was real; that there was a lot to explore both inside myself and in the outside world. And I didn't need to run away to find it. I was a model. Quitting modeling would not change anything. Most profoundly, I concluded, I liked myself for the first time in my life. I had drive, ambition, courage and character, and, heck, I was fun! Fuck it, I had idiosyncrasies, but nobody was perfect. I determined that I would quit the self-crucifixion. I'd never get shit from anyone and if I did, I'd give it back.

I explored the gay clubs that at the time where mostly on one street in the Marais. There I found myself sitting alone, drinking alone, and watching the camaraderie and friendships around me. I didn't see or understand much about social interaction. I didn't feel I knew how to make small talk and felt uncomfortable in bars regardless of their demographic.

Journal July 13: *Fears of being gay: As a Christian I would be destroying my soul. Positive factors: Meet nice people, sexually get off, being honest with my own feelings.*

One evening at a popular and comparably comfortable hangout—a loud basement bar that had a rarely used grand piano in the middle of the room—I longingly watched a beefy go-go-boy for what seemed like hours. He noticed me too. And I hoped that he—of all people—would want to make a pass at me. So I waited until the end of the night. When he finished dancing, he sat down at a table with some friends. We made more intense (and expressionless, to my understanding) stares. He did not move. I went home.

It may have been that evening, very late and the streets empty, when I was mugged. Pushed into a doorway, I felt a man grabbing for my wallet. I fought him back, held firm, kicked him and screamed "I'm an American and I'm being mugged…help, help, help." No one came to my rescue, but the man ran away. I staggered outside the building and slid to the ground delirious, confused, upset. I wasn't sure exactly where home was. Eventually it started getting light. A threesome of black men approached me (for some unexplainable reason, at the worst times of my life prior to that occasion and after, black people saved me. I knew this to be the case, and wrote of it in my later journals). The Parisians asked me how I was and what had happened. They asked where I lived and offered to walk me home. Gratefully, I accepted and they safely got me home.

Being that they were so friendly and also gay, I invited them up to my room. MK was asleep, so I asked that they all be very quiet. Still a bit delirious, I was also lonely, scared, and tired. Upon coming up to my room, one of the men sat and rested on the couch, and two others sat on my little bed with me. The three of us fooled around a bit, until it was just me and the one very pretty boy who had just gotten off his shift from McDonalds. Together we cuddled naked. It wasn't too long afterwards that the men got up and left. I never followed up with getting together with my favorite of the three—the young hamburger man—even though he gave me his number and later called.

On one of my outings of discovery at the gay bars of the Marais, I met a young and beautiful boy named Bogy. Bogy was a thin, lanky, and extremely seductive looking 21-year-old. He was a native Parisian and had an equally sultry, but somewhat meaner-looking identical twin brother. I believe that I met him in the same bar where I had been infatuated with the go-go boy, although he preferred the Banana Café next door. Vaguely it seems to me that we shared a kiss or several around the grand piano. Perhaps we did more, as MK was gone a lot—never having recovered from being embarrassed at feeling sexually rebuffed. I'm very sorry I've forgotten the events.

If it was to be homosexuality, then I wanted a boyfriend like Bogy—who I considered classical since he seemed worldly-wise, and was French. I felt he made me want to exercise, be, and act healthy— quit smoking and be as sober as I could. I prayed for him one day at a church and lit some rose incense on his behalf. I told him I believed in Jesus Christ. And I told myself that "I won't approach my relationship with him as a fucked up sort of fling…there are too many emotions involved and too many feelings can be hurt."

One afternoon he invited me over to the Banana Café where I met his brother and someone he told me was his best friend. Everyone spoke a lot but no one spoke English. And no one spoke to me. I

209

wrote that it was sad that we didn't speak the same language, but, in a way, it allowed me to separate from verbal conversation and focus on expressions and the non-verbal. I felt as if I were being inspected as I sat quietly at the table, not understanding much of their rapid and colloquial French. I took this to mean that they were determining my suitability as a boyfriend.

I liked his face and felt his body was cute. I wanted to touch him more but felt it would be a bad idea because his "best friend" was there. I sensed that he was loving and kind and at the same time, very much loved. Perhaps he was a little heart breaker, I wrote. A beautiful boy, he was also direct and had no problem in expressing himself. He knew what he had. Perhaps, I queried, he was also a bit of an opportunist.

The gay world was like "an underground society." And I was not happy about the difficulty in satisfying my needs and finding the perfect boyfriend—in Bogy or anyone else. It seemed as difficult as the search for the perfect girlfriend, if not more so since it was "undercover," and gay boys, I suspected, probably "had much more complicated lives." Still, I reiterated to my pages, I didn't want to just fuck or be fucked. I wanted love. I wanted intimacy.

One day I finally got to see Bogy and his brother's apartment. It was small, as both had very little income, but I didn't care. Memories of he and I in that room are foggy and not written down. I recall sitting in the bathroom, and Bogy giving me a massage and nothing else. I wanted so much more; I wanted him, all of him, to talk, to go farther, really be there with and for each other. But it was the height of the AIDS pandemic for Western European and U.S. gay men. I still did not know much about this, nor had I ever been tested. AIDS wasn't something I felt affected me personally, no matter that it had already been around for over a decade. Bogy was the first person who I had ever known who took precautions against it. Even though I do not recall his instructing me much on the topic, he most likely took my naiveté as strange, if not irresponsible.

For a time, he let me touch him. I later wrote in my journal "I kissed his belly and touched his whole naked body...I explored and enjoyed it." After awhile his twin brother came home. They shared the same small bed, I was told.

Although our communication was difficult, I knew that I was also invited to spend the night. My excitement was very high, believing that somehow, I would be naked and in bed with two beautiful twins, who loved each other dearly, and one who at least liked me or considered me special. I was also a bit confused. Did they have sex with each other? Did one just lay there while the other had sex? The thoughts were tantalizing, and I wanted to find out.

Apparently, I was the only one getting excited, as nothing happened. The brothers just wanted to sleep and didn't seem to be responsive to or bothered by the close proximity. I couldn't contain my hard-on, but also couldn't do anything. Eventually I went home where I could at least get some sleep.

The very next day I joined Bogy again at the Banana Café. I felt drained of all emotions for anybody except him. The feeling was not reciprocated, and I was left very unhappy. He told me that he was going to sleep with his best friend. I tried to believe that this did not affect me—that my love and compassion for him was merely brotherly.

I immediately went home and wrote extensively—mature sentences, beyond my capacity, and which I did not act upon. The pain I was feeling allowed me to have a moment of brutal honesty with myself that would once again soon be forgotten. If I had the capacity to understand my true feelings or hear my own intuition in my writings, it would have saved me further heartache, but it was, nonetheless, what I needed to experience then. I wrote that I was not in love. That instead, I was emotionally needy of male love, attention, and affection. And I was sexually repressed. What I needed was to learn how to accept myself—this included learning how to be comfortable as a piece of meat. "I know what I am; what I've done; and what I am still doing." I continued, "Everything has been my choice." My feelings were indisputably hurt. "It's all a game here," I continued, "and I'm learning to play the game." Feeling as if I were in the middle of a transition, I wrote that I wanted to be gay, was happy and challenged at being gay, but the real homosexuals weren't interested in me.

Having initiated the processing of this big realization, I once again considered my career. I was mostly positive about the decisions I needed to make. The PH1 agency had just rejected me, but I was somewhat still hopeful about modeling and even acting. Most of all I knew I didn't want to be a businessperson again. And by some driving force of insanity, I was compelled to make myself succeed. Driven "to make something happen," I determined to "keep pushing and pushing."

The following day was hot and sunny and another day of emotional and psychological recovery. I slept all day, which reminded me of the Bogy phrase "ten minutes more I go sleeping." Back in my own element for a respite, I wrote that it was funny that I was so emotionally attached to this silly 21-year-old. Having "fallen unhealthily into a love/lust relationship," I was making a fool of myself and seemed to like it. I just wanted to free myself, because I had been in love again and again with the wrong person.

But I didn't want to go through my life lonely or sad. The concept of a "normal" family life and "normal" working life was remote. Perhaps, I began to reason again, I could find a woman I could love. As the weather cooled following a mid-July patch of thunderstorms, once again I started to fall back into insecurity of who I was. I wrote a long diatribe on the unflattering root causes of my homosexuality and, less than a week after my frustrating last experience with Bogy, I took a week-long trip with Eve to the same town, Annecy, where I had my last photo shoot.

The trip was an annual one for her. She and her friends rented a decent-sized house and spent a couple weeks golfing. The group consisted of Eve and her equally professional girlfriends and their bourgeoisie husbands—lawyers, doctors, and business people. Some of the couples' babies weren't present, but the conversation swirled around family life and finances nonetheless.

One of the guests was a squat, portly Belgian lawyer with a squeaky, nasally voice, who stood out from the other preppy, handsome couples. His name was Lejeune and he was an acquaintance of mine from graduate school. Lejeune had attended the exclusive Masters of Comparative Law program with Eve, while I was completing my Masters of Business Administration. I became friends with a good group of these MCL people because I was attracted to their European-ness as opposed to my group's stodgier, although still Southern Californian, business demeanor. Adding to the fact that Lejeune was single was the fact that he was obviously extremely effeminate, in a old-school manner, much like one would imagine Oscar Wilde to be—dressed conservatively yet frilly, with a pompous, intellectual, sharp wit. The first night there, he proceeded to pour me glass after glass of expensive brandy, and the two of us got high.

Soon after retiring to our room, as was Eve's customary fashion, she "pounced" on me. I had just wanted to cuddle and before I knew it, she was sitting on me. She did the fucking, while I resented her for moving so fast. I later wrote "I felt very much like thinking of the video of homosexuality but then when I finally did cum, my mind was focused on the actual intercourse I was having with her. I had to put the thought into my mind just as it was happening. I just wasn't there for the experience." This was to be my last intercourse with a woman.

I journaled the following day that I was so isolated and lonely that I could scream. I was at a financial disadvantage to everyone and felt like Eve's paid escort. I wrote that I resented her for robbing me of my sleep—in addition to having kept me awake in order to fuck. I also resented Lejeune for getting me drunk in the first place and for not being honest with the group about being gay. Adding to a long list was that I resented my lost mobility and felt trapped.

That night, I once again smoked and drank in excess with Lejeune, while the others played Trivial Pursuit. I later described that I

213

kissed him and let him use his chubby little fingers to massage the head of my dick—although he wanted it, I didn't agree to sleep in his bed. Afterwards, I wondered when drunk, to what limit I wouldn't go.

Our conversation was, nonetheless, important to my continued development as an accepting gay person. Lejeune suggested that I wasn't comfortable with the relationship I had with my father because he probably knew I was gay (and perhaps didn't like it). Equally insightful, he told me it seemed to him that I was uncomfortable with everything about myself. If he was comfortable with the way he looked, he should assume that I be comfortable even more with my looks and myself. Why wasn't I? Was it because "I seemed to make a moral issue out of everything—smoking, homosexuality, hash—where there was none?" I wasn't sure. One thing I did know, however, was that I had a choice in who I wanted to sleep with or not.

As my torturous time progressed, I found myself mostly alone as Eve and her friends spent every day golfing and going to bed at the early hour of 11 p.m. A couple days after fucking around with Lejeune, I wrote a long list of rules by which homosexuality could be practiced. The rules included many which I would breach or already had breached such as, "no sex with multiple partners…a person's sexual activities are to be private and only necessary to be shared if that person either so chooses or feels it necessary to enlighten others because of aggressive physical or verbal instigation."

One afternoon, I had myself dropped off in a thick patch of forest nearby a great lake. Wandering amidst the trees, I felt as horny as I did on the path near the Ritz Carlton in Madrid. In a moment of erotic communing with nature, I took off all of my clothes and continued on my hike. I eventually found a shrubby private spot and jerked of in the mulch and earth. The ecstatic feelings soon left as I spent the night restless and sexless next to Eve.

Adding to this was an excruciating discomfort oozing from my ear. My prior addictive surfing had contributed to mastoiditis (infection of the temporal bone of the skull behind the ear caused by chronic middle ear infections). I had one surgery in each ear in the years immediately leading up to my trip to Europe. Since leaving for Europe, a series of infections immediately began that I did little for. Perhaps as a sign that it was time to leave not only Annecy, but Europe, one ear became badly infected (and probably had been since my exciting adventure waterskiing during the last big job I worked in the same village).

Eve, unhappy with my lack of desire, my horrific attitude towards her and her friends, and the moodiness caused by my severe physical malady, finally had enough. We quarreled, and she agreed to take me to the pharmacist and train station the very next day. A sleepless final night preceded an argument with the French pharmacist to give me the antibiotics I wanted without a prescription and a departure on the train that I was bitter about paying for.

Upon my return to Paris, I read all of my European journals from start to finish and listed what I felt were my accomplishments and failures, including that my ambitions to change the world had been set too high. Motivating this was the fact that I would soon be leaving. I had purchased a round-trip ticket from Paris to San Diego for 24 days during the August slow down. I would return to Paris at the end of August to give modeling one more try during the busy September season. According to what I figured, the IRS was supposed to deliver a check for $2,300 while I was gone, which would allow me to survive for another two to three months—I eventually left Europe broke at Christmastime 1994.

I spent my time in San Diego back in the closet, aware that I was an addict, and trying to control both. I stayed with my good friends who were kind enough to retrieve the last of my furniture from my condominium. I consoled myself with the understanding that the loss of my home represented the absence of a financial burden that I was ill suited to maintain. I visited my best surfing buddy who had invested in a cool, North County coffee house—a dream he and I had discussed during our frequent sunset surfing sessions.

I also visited Petey who unknowingly had thrown my entire world akimbo. He had gained a lot of weight to cover his writhe body. I hypothesized and secretly hoped that it was because he was trying to hide the fact that he really was gay, had been in love with me, and missed me now. We talked for an extensive period—perhaps at my surfer friend's cafe—in the setting San Diego sun about superficial subjects that I have no memory of. After this, he would disappear from San Diego and my life completely. I never found any trace of him, but looked for him in the phantom faces and characters of men that I thought I was in love with for years. After our meeting, I broke down my fractured pieces of self on paper once again—"the fearless surfer, the classical guy, the spiritual Christian, the healer and the rebel homosexual"—and determined in a drunken sprawl that instead of being both spiritual and gay, I had to choose between one or the other.

I took a set of test photos on the white sandy beaches of Coronado, 100 miles south of the successful test that started my career. I hoped that these new photos would add fuel to my gallant, successful return. I also closed down my storage unit, relieved that I no longer had to fear the potential of losing its contents for lack of payment, and moved my most prized possessions—photo albums, journals, few precious books, sculptures, drawings, and paintings—to a surfer buddy's garage attic. I called MK to find out that there was a thick envelope from the IRS, which she refused to open, but which I believed contained the money I would need. Then, taking some additional clothes and shoes that I luckily had retained, and one of the four surfboards that was still left, I wished San Diego a final goodbye.

Flying with a surfboard to Paris was an odd thing to do, but I had hopes that I would be able to surf the famous French coast and secretly excited to show my board off to Rusty. Even odder was taking the famous Metro with a wrapped up, cumbersome board. Gleefully happy that I had closure, had new clothes, and a surfboard that I hoped to be successful enough to afford a vacation with one day, I opened the letter from the IRS. To my immediate horror, the envelope contained no money—only another form that needed to be filled out with a three-month delay. Crazed, I went out to a phone booth, called my mother, and told her that God was dead—which frightened her.

In the days that followed I flew back into religiosity, and determined that I needed to "limit, decrease, and disregard any habit that brings my spirit away from the Spirit," and "cut myself free of all the demons that bring me down—hash, cigarettes and homosexual longings—or else I will not survive." I once again made a list of all the things I would have to do, which included reading the Bible, going to church, praying throughout the day, and being open and sober for what that answer was.

Wandering lost in the streets of Paris, I eventually found a new agency. Zoom had once been one of Paris' most elite agencies. It had some of the world's top models, and a reputation that was beyond reproach. But then a horrible scandal occurred, of which I never found out the details, and the agency lost all of its talent, its bookers, and its reputation. By the time I discovered them, the former head booker had set up a basic office in an old building in the outskirts of the city. He agreed to take me on. Castings were few compared to other agencies, but he did get me a job in Belgium via the Belgian agency Dominique. It turned out to be the last print job I did in Europe. I would go on to do two more television commercials in Athens before leaving Europe altogether for Christmas in Michigan and Miami Beach by New Years, 1995.

A week back from San Diego and I apparently was "glowing with the Power of the Holy Spirit—healthy, centered, not interested in drugs, cigarettes, alcohol or sex, and mellow, mellow, mellow." My renewed spiritual mood helped me get along with MK, whose moods I described as so negative and dramatic that it made me appear constantly happy. I was hanging out with Gregor again, going to the Pompidou for French lessons, and had a booker who was willing to work with me. It even seemed I was doing a good job in taking an interest in girls.

217

A friend I had made named Alesha, of whom I remember nothing, apparently knew all about Bogy and me. She also knew that I truly needed to start making more money if I were to survive. On a random Thursday in early September, she and I hung out and discussed options. A friend of hers might help get me a job as an English teacher, which would pay my rent but not much more. I indicated excitement although there was no way on earth my grandiosity could accept working on a regular basis just to pay my rent. Perhaps I could get a job at the American Bar, we thought, which seemed like a better idea. We immediately walked to this bar/restaurant where an English boy, who I found to be without compromise the most stunning boy I had ever seen, greeted me. I was overtaken by a warmth and generosity of spirit that made him blush, I later wrote. I felt our communication—which consisted of him telling me I needed to come back tomorrow when the manager was there—was so "powerful and direct" that, "when we were talking, the rest of the world seemed to disappear." I wanted to be friends with this boy. "It seems as if I know him very deeply," I wrote. And the feeling, I felt, was mutual.

My friend, noticing the interaction, asked me hypothetically, if he and I were gay, would I go for him? I responded that I wasn't going for anyone. She didn't seem to buy this and asked me how things ended with Bogy. "The jealousy, compromises, head games, power trips—the works—made it seem more difficult than a male/female relationship," I told her. Plus, I continued, all-in-all, "it made me nervous and uncomfortable." Besides, I concluded, "I didn't' fit in with his friends," and "I wasn't out to just fuck anybody...why bother?"

A couple days later, at another of MK's dinner parties, the once loathed, Beethoven-like, bisexual offered a scientific book on male homosexuality. I read the book in earnest, although it made me want to get drunk. I was able to refrain for the time being—"the good French people I'm around drink so darned moderately I am compelled to do the same," I wrote. The outcome of this cognizant period and the book was an odd experience in which I relived my experience with my father, and concluded that I was sorry for having been so angry at him; and that I truly loved him, although I never had told him so when he was alive. After my initial readings I dreamt that I was loving Bogy and "masturbating him with love."

After the dream, I immediately called Bogy and spent two hours with him. During that time, I learned that his best friend was really his boyfriend. I realized that he was using me to make his boyfriend jealous. I felt compassion instead of anger. But I no longer thought I wanted him as anything other than a friend. I couldn't take his boyfriend or his feelings for granted, or merely to satisfy my needs. The outcome of this was that I, more strongly than ever, recognized the feelings I had for him were genuine and undeniable. The type of feeling I now knew I had was in fact different from the developed relationships I had with friends back in the States. It was also different from the possibilities I had when I felt I could have a relationship with girls there. But it too developed more as the relationships grew.

My interpretation of my latest Bible readings led me to believe that I was to use my intuition and feelings as a guide—"I am guilty for doing something against God if I feel it is against him." The binding force between God, others, and myself was love. I then came to believe the feelings and type of relationship I could have with Bogy (or any man) to be moral and acceptable in the sight of God. He and I were "les enfants des Paradis." Taking this knowledge and spiritual truth into consideration, I knew that I could combine my homosexual part with my carefree, happy surfer and intellectual parts. And that I no longer need be frightened by my own nature. The very next day, I met my first boyfriend.

Madeleina-Karoline had two lipstick-lesbian friends, who were a couple, but not "out" because one worked for a high position in government and came from aristocratic parents. They were, however, "out" to a select group of "in" people. They lived together, though they maintained two fully furnished apartments—one above the other. I would soon live in one of them for a couple of weeks to save rent

219

money before I abandoned Paris altogether for the drunken debauchery that was Athens.

That mid-September Friday, they threw a party in which both sets of friends were invited—the clueless and the clued-in. MK and I were part of the "in" set and under strict rules that no hanky-panky, bisexual conversation was acceptable. We were to behave ourselves, focusing on our heterosexual sides until those that didn't know any better had all left. One of the other insiders—so inside that he was actually helping with the party—was a young and handsome, dark-haired boy named Christophe. Thin and lanky like Bogy, with a happy countenance like Scott, and the serene nature of Wim, I immediately found him extraordinarily attractive. In addition to his body, walk, spirit, and demeanor, he had a warm, delightful smile and seductive, dark, native-Parisian eyes.

Drinking little—the hostess made sure that the fine wine was served sparingly—I noticed Christophe more and more as I watched him refill glasses of wine, bring dirty dishes into the kitchen, and return with filled plates of cheese and pâté. He noticed me too, and gave me a little smile every time he passed by. MK delightedly witnessed the whole affair, completely intrigued with the potential of a real-live seduction in progress, and one that she approved of, especially since it was so *verbotten* at her girlfriends' party. MK urged that perhaps I should make my way into the kitchen when Christophe did. I noticed what seemed to be an invitation with a last-minute smile as he pushed the swing door with his foot. A little nervously, but with more vigor than usual, I followed him.

Once inside, I tried to make conversation with him. Christophe's English was minimal, and even after six months in Paris and free lessons at the Pompidou Center my French wasn't good either. But language was not on our minds as we stood near one another next to the kitchen sink. Both of our bodies spoke volumes and quite naturally we moved to engage in one of the most stimulating and impassioned kisses I ever experienced in my life.

Not long into it, however, the more bossy of the two lesbians, in her usual state of heightened awareness, walked into the kitchen. She immediately and quietly broke us apart and chastised us. We didn't care about the scolding, but out of respect for our hostess we stopped. After the regular crowd left, Christophe and I hung out with the group that remained, although our thoughts were only on the other. He eventually needed to attend to helping his friends with the clean up, and it was time for us to leave. Luckily, I had gotten his number.

I couldn't stop thinking about him but wanted to be sure not to call him too soon. Even that didn't matter, and the next day I called him. He called me back on Sunday, and we arranged a get-together at my place for Monday. I buzzed him in and then greeted him at the door, so nervous that I saw myself visibly shake. He looked good, smelled good and was extremely perceptive—"the perception of an actor studying the human being," I noted. I led him to my room, where we sat together on the little couch and talked. I had no idea what I was supposed to do or when, and wanted to make sure I didn't insult him, move too fast, or somehow misinterpret his intentions. Eventually, he leaned over and initiated the first kiss.

He took off my shirt, and we kissed and touched, my body feeling more alive than it had for as long as I could remember. From there we moved onto the floor, where the full force of our bodies rolling over one another added heat and weight to the magnetism. From the floor we moved to the bed. My pants were off and so were his, and he moved his kisses down my body and gave me a blowjob. I gave him one back.

Afterwards, I noticed myself visibly shaking once again. I later wrote that I had a rather ill feeling when I thought about what I put in my mouth, but I liked it and had wanted to experience it since the erotic dream I had of Bogy. I made dinner, and we went back at it. This time, I was the initiator from beginning to end—a fact that I felt proud of. I later wrote that I was feeling good about no longer being the victim, that I had initiated the evening: called him first; invited him to my house; began the conversation; and began the oral sex the second time.

Journal Moday, September 19: *It's a cool, drizzly day in Paris today. But for me its been a remarkable, passion filled lovely day. I made love three times from 5 or so PM until 11 Pm with a beautiful French comedian/actor/designer of 17 and 18th century costumes. We laid in each others arms. We carried on decent conversation, given his mediocre English and my mediocre French. We were sober. We were safe. We both gave much and our timing was exceptional...At first I felt nervous and uncomfortable; but in front of whom? God? Since reading Corinthians 1, I became somewhat frightened again of my homosexual nature; as if it were against God. But further readings allowed me to see Peter's attitudes about women in the church—head coverings and other formalities—which I don't believe apply. I don't believe honestly, logically, spiritually, that it is wrong for me to love a man, so long as it is discrete, honest, non-abusive, loving, and mutually agreed upon. I don't believe I will be condemned to Hell.*

The following day, I felt so good that I needed to find out if I was sane. I went to a therapist I knew about who worked for a reduced fee at the American Cathedral of Paris. There I talked about my move to Europe to become a model and my experience with Christophe, but nothing of my drinking and drugging. Of those things that I talked about, she told me everything I had longed to hear or already knew: I was perfectly sane; I had come a long way from not believing in premarital sex to actually having sex with men; my job was making me alive again; and the only thing I needed to work on was my own comfort at being assertive. My initial desire for a career change had turned out to be much more indeed, what I intuitively knew I needed that one moment when I left my last therapist in San Diego.

The days that followed left an indelible place in my memory and provided a naturally-intoxicating interlude into a genuine and new life for me. Christophe and I laughed joyously out loud as we walked up the five flights of stairs to my apartment, tearing items of clothing off one another until we were nearly naked. We didn't care what anyone thought. I lay on top of him for what seemed like hours, after simultaneous climaxing, not needing or wanting to wipe myself off.

Four days after the most intense experience in my life, I was again in my room alone, fearful of poverty and of myself. Fortunately, Christophe called, saving me from my fears, which was wonderful at the time, but also set the precedent for a dangerous pattern in future relationships. He came over, and I led the undressing, touching, and feeling. He mimicked my actions. This time we were out of synch—he came first. I later wrote this entry:

Journal September 22, 1994: *Although he is a sweetie, and a beautiful 22-year-old boy, I think this is somewhat very new for him too. I really like him and am capable of loving him. I am sexually attracted to him and get a hard-on just thinking about him. But our ages are very different. I'm 9 years older than him. And also I have feelings of guilt over my heterosexuality—I have had many hetero-experiences. I somehow still feel shaky nervous and stressed afterwards. I must free myself of any remaining constraints. I must truly be there.*

That day I concluded one of the last journal entries I was to write for several years: *I am in a good mood since masturbating and having oral sex with Christophe. There is no question about the homosexual part of my personality. At the moment I am gay and proud to be gay: I feel great about my body, mind and spirit.*

Acknowledgements

I thank you, Mike, for your support, encouragement, and work on this book. You were there to listen and your perception was invaluable. Thank you for your understanding as you loved me through my processing boundless personal nostalgia.

I recognize my father, who supported me emotionally, financially, and spiritually throughout his life and beyond. It was his dream to retire on a white, sandy beach. When he died, I was able to move to San Diego, get my MBA, and buy a home near the beach with his inheritance. He believed in experiencing life to its fullest, which needless to say, comes with inherent risk. Thank you, Dad.

I thank Mom and Omi, whose wish for me was a stable, abundant, and less risky life. I know that my trials tested you as well, Mom. Thank you for loving me. And, by the way, thanks for managing the nightmare that was my bills.

Gratitude to John Reeder for his continual support, encouragement, and sponsorship. I thank my editor, Toni Kelley, for her superb work, which included much more than just punctuation. Also due my gratitude is Jennifer Cunningham, who took the time to read my original and final drafts and whose garage I stored my personal possessions in for five years (thank you, Steve, too!). Note: her mother was the Hewlett-Packard personnel manager with whom I left my termination voicemail and who kindly called me back.

Finally, I thank the countless co-workers, models, agents, bookers, clients, photographers and friends whom I gained and lost. I appreciate all of you for helping me learn the lessons that I am here to experience.

All of you, deceased and alive, I wish Love and Light.

ALSO BY ROBERT N. REINCKE

Death of a Past Life

CPSIA information can be obtained
at www.ICGtesting.com
Printed in the USA
BVHW070819080120
568938BV00024B/1171/P